Trader Vic's Book of
Mexican Cooking

Trader Vic's Book of
Mexican
Cooking

VICTOR J. BERGERON

DRAWINGS BY CHERYL OLSEN

DOUBLEDAY & CO., INC.
GARDEN CITY, NEW YORK

Color photographs 1, 2, 3 and 8 by Bruce Harlow, the balance by Robert Gries

ISBN: 0-385-01748-0
Library of Congress Catalog Card Number 72–96228
Copyright © 1973 by Doubleday & Company, Inc.
All Rights Reserved
Printed in the United States of America
First Edition

To Leonora Wood of Refugio, Texas

Foreword

You have to have a reason to write a book. That's what it says. Well, I have had a mad on for Mexican food for a thousand years. When Mr. Roth purchased the Ghirardelli Chocolate Factory and turned it into what is now the famous Ghirardelli Square here in San Francisco, he asked me if I would open a Mexican restaurant there. At that time I knew as much about Mexican food as my great-grandmother in the Pyrenees Mountains in France. So, when you don't know anything about something, you go and learn about it.

I ate Mexican food until it almost gave me an ulcer. In Mexico it was pretty greasy. The finest Mexican food I have enjoyed came from what is known as Texas-Mex. Now, I know I'm going to make a lot of Mexicans sore as hell—you have to understand that I am an American, not a Mexican, and I eat what pleases me most.

So, my wife and I went to work flying all over Mexico, eating their stuff, and then making adjustments on it so it would be palatable to Americans. You will see in these recipes throughout this book.

One thing I do want to say about the Mexicans—they do a terrific job in the homecraft industry. All over Mexico there are these wonderful things to buy which are absolutely the most. Everything in our Señor Pico restaurants in Ghirardelli Square and Century City, Los Angeles, was handcrafted in Mexico and hand-selected by me and my wife.

After Doubleday published my *Pacific Island Cookbook*, in which there were some recipes from Mexico and Texas, the response to the book was great because of the growing interest in Mexican cuisine, and Doubleday asked me to devote an entire book to Mexican food. Here it is.

I hope you will enjoy these recipes as much as I have had fun in writing them for you.

Contents

Recipes for items that are capitalized in the text can be located in the Index.

Introduction

The introduction is supposed to introduce the people to the thing we are writing about, so I guess we have to tell you a little bit about Mexico, which you most likely already know.

Maybe as many as thousands of years ago people started coming across the Bering Sea and maybe some by boat from Europe and landed all over the Americas and great civilizations developed, for some unknown reason, in Mexico.

Mayans and, of course, the Aztecs created magnificent cities comparable in every way to those of the Romans and the Egyptians.

In Bernal Díaz del Castillo's Book, *The True History of the Conquest of New Spain,* which I think is the best book to read, it tells about the fantastic food that Montezuma ate and served at his table, sometimes as many as fifteen or twenty varieties, all new taste delights for the Spaniards who conquered Mexico. There was corn, the Mexican's staff of life; and chilies, his spice of life. There were beans of every shape and size and color to round out the basic staples of his diet. And there was one new taste delight after another of chocolate, vanilla, pineapple, papaya, tomatoes, avocados, eggplant, squash, sweet potatoes, peanuts, and cashews.

The Spaniards were even more astonished to find the Aztec cuisine so highly sophisticated. Every meal was composed of many different dishes, bland and spicy flavors were imaginatively combined, cooked foods were kept hot over small pottery braziers, and everything was beautifully presented to please the eye as well as the palate.

In time, Spain made important contributions to the native foods of Mexico, adding rice, wheat, and potatoes, olive oil and wine, onions and garlic, and cinnamon and cloves. Later, ships brought plantings for vineyards and for orchards of peaches, apricots, almonds, and pine nuts. Also from Spain came chickens and then livestock, providing pork and lard as well as beef, milk, and butter.

The Spaniards, of course, introduced many of their dishes to Mexico. Three centuries later, during the short reign of Maximilian, many French, Austrian, and Italian dishes were introduced. While Mexican cuisine has been influenced over the past centuries by these many different cultures, it has never been dominated by any one of them. Mexican dishes are still distinctively Mexican. For which I say, Amen.

During the last fifteen years or so, the popularity of Mexican foods has taken a tremendous spurt here in the States. Mexican restaurants are springing up here, there, and everywhere. Mexican grocery stores are plentiful in our urban areas. Even our supermarkets are now well stocked with many fine canned, packaged, and frozen Mexican foods. And thousands of travelers are returning from vacations South of the Border determined to add the art of Mexican cooking to their culinary skills.

This cookbook can help you do just that—and without a lot of fuss and bother, because I don't believe in doing things the hard way if there's an easy way to do them. Even in Mexico, primitive utensils and laborious methods of food preparation are a thing of the past except among the very poor in the rural areas of the country. If you have an electric blender, as many Mexican housewives now have, you can whip up a Mexican meal in the same time as you can cook in any other language.

As in all countries, the family menus in Mexico are dependent on the family budget, but it is only the very poor of the country whose daily diet is confined to tortillas, chilies, and beans. By contrast, the middle-class Mexican housewife serves her family a wide variety of interesting dishes and a very substantial *comida,* the main meal of the day. In the homes of the wealthy, the menus are as Continental as they are in Mexico's fine restaurants and luxury hotels. In these homes, if Mexican appetizers are served with cocktails, or the meal includes one or more Mexican dishes, it is simply a matter of preference rather than custom.

While Mexican cuisine is lively and spirited, it is not necessarily hot and fiery. Chilies come in all degrees of heat from mild to zippy to "watch-out," but you can temper the seasoning to suit your own taste buds by using a light hand with these peppers. After all, no two Mexicans ever cook the same dish quite the same way. These people are very inventive in the kitchen and they couldn't care less about rules and regulations when it comes to cooking. If they can add and subtract from the kettle, so can you.

At any rate, this is not a book for the purist. Wherever possible, I've simplified these recipes to save you time and trouble. Canned ingredients have been substituted for fresh whenever the finished dish will taste just as good. And most important, I've adjusted flavors to suit the American palate—which is something I've learned through my restaurant experience.

13

The recipes in this book have come from practically all over hell's half acre. Some are from my Señor Pico restaurants, others were gathered on my travels throughout Mexico, and many came from friends of mine who are descendants of pioneer families in Texas, New Mexico, and California. From a church in Brownsville, Texas, I was given permission to reprint some exceptionally good recipes from a collection of recipes donated by its congregation. And I am especially indebted for some great ideas and recipes to Leonora Wood, of Refugio, Texas, and an old friend, Kay Witherspoon, of Albuquerque, New Mexico—two gals who really know their Mexican food.

Trader Vic's Book of
Mexican Cooking

The Corn-Based Foods of Mexico

Tortillas
Enchiladas
Tamales

Corn is to Mexico what wheat is to North America—the staff of life. The best known Mexican dishes—the tortillas, tacos, enchiladas, and tamales—are all made with Mexican corn flour (not to be confused with our corn meal).

In ancient times, it was one helluva job to make this flour. The corn had to be dried, then boiled with lime to make *nixtamal.* Then the nixtamal had to be ground, on a flat stone with a stone rolling pin, into flour from which to make the *masa,* the dough used for making tortillas and the other corn-based Mexican foods.

Today, this Mexican corn flour, called *masa harina,* is available at all Mexican grocery stores. Masa harina is also marketed by Quaker Oats and can be found in many of our specialty food stores and supermarkets.

TORTILLAS

The tortilla is the native bread of modern Mexico, just as it was in ancient times before the Spaniards introduced wheat to the country.

This flat pancake shows up at every Mexican meal in some form or another and in between meals as well. Served as bread, the tortilla is usually made in a large, six-inch circle. Wrapped around a filling and cooked in a sauce, it becomes an enchilada. A small four-inch tortilla, soft-fried and cupped around a filling, becomes a taco; crisp-fried, a tostada. Tiny two- and three-inch tortillas are used in many different ways for appetizers at cocktail parties. These are called *antojitos,* and their recipes are included in this chapter.

Tamales are something else again and not at all like a tortilla. But because they also require masa harina as an ingredient, they are included in this chapter.

There are many more traditional Mexican dishes made with tortillas in some form or another, and you'll find a good sampling of them on the following pages.

Corn Flour Tortillas

While you can buy good, ready-to-heat-and-eat, canned or frozen tortillas at most supermarkets, they're kind of fun to make and you may get a big kick out of turning out your own. You can either shape the masa (dough) by hand, as many Mexican cooks still do, or you can use an inexpensive tortilla press, which is available in most Mexican stores. Or you can use the easy method suggested in the following recipe. Tortillas are baked like a pancake on the top of the stove. In Mexico, they use a large, flat earthenware disc, called a *comal*, but a regular pancake griddle or a cast-iron skillet will do just as well.

TORTILLA DOUGH

2 cups masa harina
1 teaspoon salt
1 to 1⅓ cups warm water

In a mixing bowl, combine the masa harina and salt; gradually add the water, stirring constantly. Mix well with your hands until the dough no longer sticks to your fingers. (If the dough is too moist, add a little more masa harina; it won't hurt the dough to handle it.)

Divide the dough into 12 balls about the size of an egg. Flatten by pressing between sheets of wax paper, using a tortilla press or the flat bottom of a baking dish. Press the tortillas into thin 4½- to 5-inch circles, about ⅟₁₆ of an inch thick.

Heat an ungreased griddle or cast-iron skillet over moderate heat and cook the tortillas, one at a time, for about 2 minutes on each side or until the edges begin to lift and the bottom has become a delicate brown. Adjust the heat if the tortillas brown too fast. Stack the tortillas as they are made and wrap 4 or 5 at a time in foil to keep them warm in the oven until serving. This recipe makes 1 dozen small tortillas.

To keep tortillas warm:

You can make corn tortillas ahead and keep them warm for as long as 2 or 3 hours in a preheated 200° F. oven. Wrap stacks of 4 in paper toweling, then in a well-dampened cloth, then in foil before placing them in the oven. Check along the way and redampen the cloth if necessary.

To reheat corn tortillas:

Lightly brush each side with water, then place the tortilla flat on an ungreased griddle or skillet over medium heat, turning frequently, until soft and pliable. It only takes about 20 to 30 seconds.

To soft-fry corn tortillas:

Heat about ¼ inch oil in a frying pan over medium heat. Fry the tortillas, one at a time, turning frequently, until softened. It only takes about 10 to 15 seconds. Be careful not to cook them too long or over too high heat or they will fry crisp. As each tortilla is finished, drain it on paper towels.

White Flour Tortillas

You can buy tortillas made of white flour as well as the regular Mexican corn tortillas from Mexican grocery stores or, sometimes, in the freezing departments of the larger markets. If you can't find them, you can make your own. Make them in small batches at a time for easier handling.

These are really good tasting when freshly made and hot. They're soft, as well, when freshly made, and can be used in place of corn tortillas for enchiladas and other recipes.

2 cups all-purpose flour
1 teaspoon salt
2½ tablespoons lard
Lukewarm water

Sift flour and salt together; cut in the lard and stir in the water gradually, enough to form a soft but firm dough. Divide into 6 balls about 2 inches in diameter and let rest on a floured pastry board for about 20 minutes. Roll balls out as thin as possible—about 1/16 of an inch thick—and cut into 6-inch rounds.

You can use a plate as a pattern and cut around it with a knife. Bake on an ungreased griddle or skillet over moderate flame for 2 minutes on each side, turning with a pancake turner. The tortillas should bake through but not brown. Stack and wrap in a clean cloth, then put in a plastic film bag until ready to use. Makes 8 large tortillas.

To reheat flour tortillas:

Lightly brush tortillas on each side with a drop or two of water; place in a covered ovenproof dish or wrap in foil. Heat in a preheated 300° F. oven for 10 to 15 minutes.

ENCHILADAS

Enchiladas are tortillas with fillings of meat, cheese, or chicken combined with other ingredients. They are rolled, covered with sauce, and baked until heated through. The sauces are usually highly seasoned and made either with a tomato base and dried red chilies or with green chilies or Mexican green tomatoes.

A Mexican-style meal of enchiladas can be put together in minutes if you keep tortillas in the freezer and sauce in the refrigerator. The traditional accompaniments are easy if you have instant rice and canned refried beans on hand. The filling combinations can be varied; for instance, a mixture of cream cheese, chopped poblano chilies, chopped black olives, and chopped canned chicken. Pork can be used in place of chicken or beef. Avocados go great with shrimp, onions, and chili powder, or you can use *guacamole* with chicken or shrimp. After you enjoy these recipes, experiment on your own. Try something different!

Señor Pico Cheese Enchiladas

> 2 cups cottage cheese
> 1 pound New York white Cheddar, shredded
> ¼ cup chopped cooked onions
> ¼ cup crushed tostadas (see Index) or packaged tortilla chips
> 2 tablespoons chopped olives
> 2 tablespoons chopped jalapeño chilies
> 1 teaspoon salt
> 1 teaspoon monosodium glutamate
> 12 tortillas
> Oil for frying
> Red or Green Enchilada Sauce (recipes follow)

Mix cheeses, onions, tostadas, olives, and chilies; add seasonings. Soft-fry the tortillas in oil until soft and pliable—not crisp. Drain and dip into whichever sauce is being used, coating both sides completely. Place filling in center of prepared tortillas and roll them up. Place in greased baking dish with overlapped edges down and top with either Red or Green Enchilada Sauce.

If you are using Red Enchilada Sauce, pour heated sauce over enchiladas and top with grated Cheddar cheese. Bake in a preheated 350° F. oven until thoroughly heated and cheese has melted. Makes 6 servings, allowing 2 per person.

If you are using Green Enchilada Sauce, pour sauce over enchiladas without topping of cheese and bake in moderate oven until piping hot. Top with sour cream *after* removing enchiladas from oven.

RED ENCHILADA SAUCE

> ¼ cup chopped onions
> 1 clove garlic, minced
> 2 tablespoons oil

2 cans boiling chicken broth
1 tablespoon chili powder
¼ cup flour
1 teaspoon salt or to taste
2 teaspoons monosodium glutamate
1 tablespoon oil
1 small (10-ounce) can Las Palmas Red Chili Sauce

Sauté onions and garlic together in the oil. When onions are transparent, add to boiling broth. Mix all other ingredients with the Las Palmas Red Chili Sauce to make a heavy paste. Reduce with some of the broth to pouring consistency, to avoid the possibility of lumping, and gradually stir into the hot broth. Stir for 5 minutes, then let simmer for another 10 minutes. Makes about 1 quart of sauce.

GREEN ENCHILADA SAUCE

2 cans Campbell's Cream of Mushroom Soup
1 3½-ounce can Ortega green chilies, rinsed, seeded,
    and cut up
1 large onion, chopped
1 clove garlic, minced
1 can chicken broth
½ cup puréed raw spinach
½ teaspoon salt
1 teaspoon monosodium glutamate
2 tablespoons flour
½ pint sour cream

Purée mushroom soup, chilies, onion, and garlic in blender. Add to chicken broth and bring to a boil. Add puréed spinach and seasonings; reduce heat and let simmer for 10 to 15 minutes. Mix the flour with a little cold water to a smooth paste and stir into the sauce; bring to a boil, stirring constantly to thicken without lumping. Reduce heat and simmer for 5 minutes, continuing to stir. Correct seasonings, pour over cheese enchiladas, and bake in a preheated 350° F. oven until piping hot. Top with sour cream before serving. Recipe makes about 1 quart of sauce.

Chicken Enchiladas with Chili Sauce

> 4 cups diced cooked chicken
> ½ pound Cheddar cheese, grated
> 1 pint sour cream
> 12 tortillas
> Oil for frying
> Chili Sauce (recipe follows)

Combine chicken meat, grated cheese, and sour cream. Soft-fry the tortillas in the oil, one at a time, then dip in the heated chili sauce. Fill each sauced tortilla with chicken mixture and roll it up. Place rolls close together in a greased flat casserole, overlapped side down, and pour remaining sauce over them. Bake in a preheated 350° F. oven for about 20 minutes or until thoroughly heated. Makes 6 servings, allowing 2 tortillas per serving.

CHILI SAUCE

> 2 onions, finely chopped
> 1 clove garlic, minced
> 2 tablespoons oil
> 1½ cups canned green chilies, rinsed, seeded, and
>   chopped
> 5 ripe tomatoes, peeled and chopped
> Pinch of orégano
> 1 teaspoon salt
> ¼ teaspoon pepper

Sauté onions and garlic in oil until transparent and limp. Add chopped chilies and tomatoes, orégano, salt, and pepper. Cook over low heat, stirring occasionally, until mixture thickens. Makes about 4 cups sauce.

Chicken Enchiladas—No. 2

4½ cups coarsely chopped cooked chicken
½ cup cooked chopped onions
¼ cup chopped ripe olives
4 cups Red Enchilada Sauce (see Index)
2 teaspoons salt
2 teaspoons monosodium glutamate
12 tortillas
Oil for frying
1½ cups grated Cheddar cheese

Combine the first 3 ingredients with 1 cup of the Red Enchilada Sauce. Stir in the salt and monosodium glutamate and mix well. Heat the remaining 3 cups of sauce and keep warm. Soft-fry the tortillas (do not let them get crisp); drain on paper towels, then dip into the warm sauce, coating both sides completely.

Put about a ½ cup of filling in each tortilla, roll up, and place, overlapped side down, in a greased baking dish. Bake in a preheated 375° F. oven for about 20 minutes or until heated through. Meanwhile, reheat sauce. When enchiladas are hot, spoon sauce over them and sprinkle each with 2 tablespoons grated Cheddar cheese. Makes 6 servings, allowing 2 enchiladas per person.

Beef Enchiladas

Simply substitute coarsely chopped, cooked beef for the chicken in the preceding recipe for chicken enchiladas.

Ground Beef Enchiladas

If you are inspired to make enchiladas on a sudden impulse and have no cooked beef on hand, here is a recipe using ground beef.

1½ pounds ground beef
¾ cup chopped onions
3 tablespoons oil
3 cups Red Enchilada Sauce, heated (see Index)
Pinch of cuminseed
2 teaspoons salt
2 teaspoons monosodium glutamate
12 tortillas
Oil for frying
¼ cup chopped ripe olives
1½ cups grated Cheddar cheese

Sauté meat and onions in the oil until meat is crumbly and the onions are limp; add 1½ cups of the Red Enchilada Sauce, the cumin, salt, and monosodium glutamate and let simmer for 30 minutes. Meanwhile, soft-fry the tortillas in oil, drain on paper towels, then dip each one into the remaining heated Enchilada Sauce, coating both sides thoroughly. Now add the ripe olives to the cooked meat and divide mixture among the 12 tortillas. Roll up the tortillas and place them, overlapped side down, in a greased baking dish. Spoon the balance of the Enchilada Sauce over the enchiladas and bake in a preheated 375° F. oven for 20 minutes. Remove from oven and sprinkle with grated cheese. Serve with Refried Beans. Makes 6 servings, allowing 2 enchiladas per serving.

Burritos

8 white flour tortillas
1 onion, minced

1 tablespoon oil
4 cups canned refried beans
¼ head lettuce, shredded
1 large tomato, peeled and sliced
1 avocado, peeled and sliced
8 green onions, chopped
1 cup shredded cheese, Monterey Jack or Cheddar
Taco Sauce (see Index)

Place tortillas in ovenproof dish, sprinkle with a teaspoon of water; cover and heat for 10 minutes in a preheated 300° F. oven. Sauté onion in oil, add beans and heat through. Put a large spoonful of beans in the center of each tortilla, top with lettuce, tomato and avocado slices, green onions, cheese, and Taco Sauce. Fold the tortilla over the filling, at sides and ends, to enclose the filling completely. Put burritos in a baking pan and heat in a preheated 350° F. oven for about 10 minutes. Serve immediately. Makes 4 servings, allowing 2 burritos per person.

Texas-Mex Envueltos

The difference between enchiladas and envueltos seems to be a mere technicality.

1 pound ground beef
2 tablespoons oil
1 clove garlic, minced
½ teaspoon crushed cuminseed
1 teaspoon salt
¼ teaspoon pepper
24 tortillas, fried soft
Envueltos Sauce (recipe follows)
½ cup shredded Cheddar cheese

Brown meat in oil with garlic, add cuminseed, salt, and

pepper, and cook until done. Divide cooked meat mixture into centers of soft-fried tortillas and roll tightly. Place in greased casserole, overlapped side down. Pour sauce over rolled tortillas, cover, and bake for 30 minutes in a preheated 350° F. oven. To serve, sprinkle with grated Cheddar cheese. Makes 12 servings, allowing 2 envueltos per person.

ENVUELTOS SAUCE

1 onion, chopped
½ large green pepper, chopped
2 stalks celery, chopped
2 tablespoons oil
1 No. 2 can solid pack tomatoes, chopped
1 large bottle stuffed green olives, chopped
2 canned pimientos, chopped
¼ teaspoon pepper

Sauté the onion, green pepper, and celery in the oil. Add the tomatoes and simmer until tomatoes have disintegrated. Chop and add olives, pimientos, and pepper. Let mixture cook over low heat for 15 minutes, then pour over rolled tortillas.

Texas-Mex Chilaquiles

1 onion, chopped
1 clove garlic, minced
2 tablespoons oil
2 cups canned tomatoes
1 teaspoon salt
¼ teaspoon pepper
1 3½-ounce can Ortega chilies, rinsed, seeded, and
    cut into strips
12 packaged or homemade tortillas
Oil for frying

1 pound Cheddar cheese, grated
½ pint sour cream

Sauté onion and garlic in oil until transparent; add tomatoes, salt, and pepper, and simmer for 10 or 15 minutes, breaking up the tomatoes. Add the chilies; let simmer while you prepare tortillas. Cut tortillas into triangles and fry quickly until crisp in hot oil. Remove immediately. Arrange a layer of fried tortillas (tostadas) in well-greased casserole, then a layer of the sauce and a thick layer of grated cheese. Continue in this manner until dish is filled, ending with grated cheese. Bake in a preheated 350° F. oven for 30 minutes. Just before serving, cover top with sour cream and return to oven until sour cream is heated. Makes 6 to 8 servings.

Chilaquile Pie

This recipe came to me labeled "Tamale Pie," but it really is an Americanized version of *chilaquiles*, a true Mexican dish made up of alternating layers of pieces of tortillas, a sauce consisting of serrano chilies, green tomatoes, coriander, white onions, and layers of grated cheese. Frankly, I like this recipe better than the more authentic version.

¼ cup oil
1 large onion, chopped
1 green pepper, chopped
2 pounds ground beef
2 teaspoons chili powder
½ teaspoon orégano
¼ teaspoon garlic powder
2 teaspoons salt
¼ teaspoon black pepper
1 No. 2½ can Las Palmas Red Chili Sauce
1 No. 2 can whole kernel corn

1 small can pitted black olives, or more
Oil for frying
10 soft tortillas
1 pound Tillamook cheese, grated
Chopped green onions
Sprigs of parsley
Sliced radishes

Heat the oil in a large skillet, add the onion and green pepper and sauté until onion is transparent. Add beef and stir-fry until meat is crumbly and has lost its red color. Add seasonings and let simmer for a few seconds to develop flavor, then add chili sauce, corn, and olives. Cover and simmer for 30 minutes. Meanwhile, cut the tortillas into ¼- to ½-inch strips and fry them in oil, a few strips at a time, without browning; let drain on paper towels. When meat mixture is ready, start with a double layer of tortilla pieces in the bottom of a well-greased large casserole and alternate layers of tortillas, meat mixture, and grated cheese, ending with cheese on top. Bake uncovered in a preheated 350° F. oven for 45 minutes. To serve, garnish with chopped green onions, sprigs of parsley, and sliced radishes. Makes 8 to 10 servings.

Señor Pico Tamales

Tamales are probably the best known of all Mexican dishes, although I think we eat more of them in the States than they do South of the Border. In Mexico, unfilled tamales are sometimes eaten as bread with certain dishes, sweet tamales are eaten as desserts, and tiny ones as appetizers. If you live where you can buy the prepared masa, corn husks, and other Mexican specialties, there is no reason why you can't have fun making your own. And you might as well make a big batch of them, if you have a freezer. They can be frozen and steamed as needed.

The procedure is to buy the prepared coarse tamale masa

and prepare it for lining the corn husks. Then the filling is put in the center of each husk, the husks are rolled firmly and tied. Here are the ingredients and instructions for 35 medium-sized tamales the way we make them at Señor Pico's.

2–2¼ pounds corn husks
1 pound lard
7 pounds coarse tamale masa
3 tablespoons salt
2 tablespoons monosodium glutamate
1 tablespoon chili powder
1 cup canned Las Palmas Red Chili Sauce
1 cup chicken broth
Tamale filling (recipe follows)

Separate and clean any stray corn silk from husks. Soak in hot water for 30 minutes or until softened; drain and pat dry with paper towels. Place lard in mixing bowl and whip at high speed until light and airy; gradually add the prepared masa, then salt, monosodium glutamate, chili powder, chili sauce, and chicken broth. Beat to the consistency of whipped cream. Test masa by placing a spoonful in cold water. If it floats to the surface, it is ready for the tamale preparation. Lay husks, about 2 for each tamale, according to size, tip to base and base to tip, reversing them as needed. With a spatula, spread the masa into a ⅛-inch-thick rectangle, about 3 by 4 inches. The masa should reach almost to the long sides of the husk, leaving the tip and base bare. Place filling in center of masa-lined husks, then roll together firmly. Tie ends securely with raffia or string. Cut off excess husks to make a neat tamale.

FILLING FOR SEÑOR PICO TAMALES

½ pound ground pork
¼ cup oil
1 clove garlic, minced

¼ cup finely chopped onions
1 cup chicken stock
1 small can tomato paste
2 teaspoons salt
2 teaspoons monosodium glutamate
2 teaspoons chili powder
1 10-ounce can Las Palmas Red Chili Sauce
½ cup tamale masa
¼ cup flour
2 cups diced boiled beef or other meat
Salt-cured black olives, pitted

Sauté pork in oil, add garlic and onions, and cook until transparent and limp. In a saucepan, heat chicken stock, add pork and onion mixture, tomato paste, seasonings, and chili sauce. Let simmer for 15 to 20 minutes to develop flavor. Combine the masa and the flour with enough cold water to make a smooth, loose paste. Use this to thicken the mixture in the saucepan, stirring constantly, to make a smooth, thick sauce. Add beef and then let cool. Put 2 heaping spoonfuls of meat and sauce on prepared husks, add 2 salt-cured black olives, roll tamale, and tie. Lay the tamales, seam side down, in layers on a rack and steam above gently boiling water in a tightly closed steamer for 1 hour. Makes enough filling for 35 medium-sized tamales.

NOTE: Diced cooked turkey or chicken, or a mixture of both, or veal may be substituted for the beef. A Picadillo Filling may also be used, just as it is for taquitos. (See recipe in the chapter on antojitos.)

TAMALITOS

Should you have more tamale filling than you need, make tiny tamales, using small husks, prepared the same way as for the large ones. Spread masa on husks, add filling, and roll together firmly. Tie ends with raffia or string. These may be steamed for immediate use or frozen and steamed when needed. To serve, steam for half an hour, snip off one end and serve hot with cocktails. Guests take a bite and scrape the filling into their mouths, something like eating an artichoke leaf.

Kay's Pork Tamale Pie

This is one of many recipes in this book from my good friend, Kay Witherspoon, who lived in Mexico for a number of years and who knows Mexican cooking like a native. Kay says that "real" Mexican tamales are made with pork, unlike the beef and chicken so often favored here in the States. Anyway, here's Kay's version of a "real" Mexican tamale pie. It's a pip, but if you prefer beef to pork, see the recipe after this one.

> 2 pounds lean boneless pork, cubed
> 2 medium-large onions, diced
> 1 clove garlic, minced
> ½ teaspoon orégano
> 1 teaspoon salt
> 4½ cups water
> 1 cup white corn meal
> 1 cup masa harina
> 1 tablespoon lard
> ½ cup diced green olives
> ½ cup raisins, softened in hot water
> 1 No. 2 can tomatoes
> 1 tablespoon chili powder
> ¼ teaspoon powdered cumin
> Grated Parmesan or Cheddar cheese

Place the pork in a heavy saucepan with one half of the diced onions, the garlic, orégano, and salt in the 4½ cups water. Cover the pan, bring to a boil, then reduce heat and simmer until meat is tender (about 1½ hours or so). Remove the meat when tender, shred it, and set aside. Strain the broth, reserving the liquid, and let it cool.

Add sufficient water to the cooled liquid, if needed, to make 4 cups. Mix in the corn meal and masa harina and bring to a boil. Let boil, stirring constantly, until thickened. When mixture is thick and while still hot, beat in the tablespoon of lard with a rotary beater for about 5 minutes until the "mush" is fluffy. Line a 2-quart casserole (that has a cover) with half of the mush, bringing it up on the sides; set aside.

Now combine the remaining ingredients, except for the cheese, in a saucepan, add the shredded meat and the reserved diced onions, and cook over medium heat until well blended and mixture is hot. Pour the hot meat mixture into the mush-lined casserole; top with the remaining mush. Sprinkle on a generous amount of grated cheese, cover the casserole, and bake in a preheated 350° F. oven for about 30 minutes or until bubbly hot. Makes 8 servings.

NOTE: This tamale pie can be made the night before serving and kept refrigerated until you are ready to bake it in the oven. Bring the casserole to room temperature before baking.

Kay's Beef Tamale Pie

> 1 pound ground lean beef
> 1 large onion, chopped
> 1 tablespoon oil
> 2 roasted green chilies (see Index)
> 1 4½-ounce can ripe olives, pitted and diced
> ½ teaspoon orégano
> 2 teaspoons chili powder
> 1 No. 2 can tomatoes
> Salt to taste
> ½ cup masa harina
> ½ cup hominy grits

1 cup white corn meal
1 teaspoon salt
4 cups cold water
1 tablespoon lard
1 small can tomato sauce for topping

In a large skillet, sauté the meat and the onion in the oil until onion is tender and the redness is gone from the meat. Drain off any excess fat. Add the next 6 ingredients and simmer over very low heat for about 10 minutes until flavors are well blended.

While meat mixture is simmering prepare the "mush" mixture and the lining of the casserole as directed in the previous recipe for Kay's Pork Tamale Pie.

Pour the meat mixture into the mush-lined casserole. Top with the remaining mush. Pour on the tomato sauce. Cover the casserole and bake in a preheated 350° F. oven for about 30 minutes or until bubbly hot.

Tacos and other Antojitos

ANTOJITOS

This word comes from the Spanish and means little whims, fancies, or desires. Here in the States, we'd say appetizers or snacks to describe the same thing. But whatever you want to call the finger foods, the dips, and all the other goodies you munch on between meals and with cocktails—that's what the following recipes are all about.

Tacos are the best known of all the antojitos and one of

Mexico's most delightful between-meal snacks, found at bus stops, lunch counters, and roadside stands throughout the country. A taco is a small tortilla folded and fried (soft-fried or crisp-fried) then filled with meat or chicken, garnished with sauce, shredded lettuce, sliced radishes, and grated sharp cheese. The Mexicans sometimes fill their tacos and then fry them, but I think this makes them too greasy. I like my tacos fried crisp into a proper shape, drained on paper towels and then filled. You can stand the taco shells in a pan in the oven to keep warm and use as needed. If you want to prepare tacos for company, serve bowls of garnishes and sauce on the side and let your guests help themselves to these finishing touches. They're great with cold beer. While the fillings most often used are beef or chicken, you can use refried beans with onions, enchilada fillings if they are a little on the dry side, or Picadillo Filling (see recipe following Taquitos in this chapter).

Beef Tacos

2 4-inch links (½ cup, if homemade) chorizo sausages
1 large onion, chopped
2 tablespoons oil
1 pound ground beef
1 teaspoon chili powder
2 tablespoons white vinegar
1 teaspoon salt
¼ teaspoon pepper
2 cups Red or Green Enchilada Sauce (see Index)
12 4-inch tortillas*
Oil for frying
Garnishes (given below)

Peel and crumble chorizos. Sauté onion in oil until limp, add chorizos and beef, and sauté until beef is crumbly and has lost its redness. Drain off excess fat. Add chili powder, vinegar, salt, and pepper. Stir well and let simmer for a few minutes. Add

Red or Green Enchilada Sauce, mix well, cover, and let simmer for about 1 hour. Meanwhile, fry each tortilla in oil and quickly fold. Dip in hot oil again, holding the tortilla with tongs. Remove and let cool. As they cool, they should become crisp. When meat mixture has simmered for an hour, remove cover and let cook until almost dry. Fill fried tacos and let your guests help themselves to the garnishes. Makes 12 filled tacos.

* Packaged tacos can be purchased in many markets ready to heat and fill.

GARNISHES

    1½ cups shredded lettuce
    1 cup grated Cheddar cheese
    ½ cup sliced radishes
    1 cup Salsa Cruda (see Index)

Chicken Tacos

    1 large onion, finely chopped
    2 tablespoons oil
    2 cups coarsely chopped cooked chicken
    1 cup Red Enchilada Sauce (see Index)
    ½ teaspoon salt
    12 tacos (4-inch tortillas), fried and shaped

Sauté onions in oil until limp; add chopped chicken and mix well. Add Red Enchilada Sauce and salt; let simmer until mixture is almost dry. Fill prepared tacos and garnish as for beef tacos in preceding recipe. Makes 6 servings, allowing 2 tacos per serving.

Taquitos

Some delicious and interesting hors d'oeuvres can be made from small soft tortillas, about 2½ to 3 inches in diameter. Taquitos, meaning little tacos, are one of them. Put one teaspoon of picadillo filling (given below) in the center of each little tortilla, fold over, and skewer together with a toothpick. Lightly deep-fry in oil; they shouldn't be too crisp. While the following recipe would provide the filling for 120 to 125 taquitos, the picadillo will keep and may be served as a main dish course accompanied by rice or beans. You can also prepare extra taquitos and freeze them for future use.

PICADILLO FILLING FOR TAQUITOS

¼ pound ground beef
¼ pound ground pork
2 tablespoons minced onions
2 tablespoons oil
1 cup peeled, chopped tomatoes
1 clove garlic, minced
3 tablespoons wine vinegar
1 tablespoon sugar
½ teaspoon ground cumin
½ teaspoon salt
½ teaspoon monosodium glutamate
2 tablespoons seedless raisins
1 tablespoon flour
2 tablespoons blanched, slivered almonds
2 tablespoons crushed walnuts

In a skillet, sauté meat and onions in a little oil until onions are transparent. Add remaining ingredients except for the nuts, and stir well to blend. Cover and simmer for half an hour, stirring occasionally. Stir in the nuts last. Taste and correct seasonings. Let cool. Makes about 2½ cups picadillo.

Señor Pico Quesadillas

This next hors d'oeuvre calls for flour tortillas cut in quarters and folded (like the old-fashioned diaper) over a cheese filling. You could actually use regular corn tortillas or pie pastry the same way.

> ½ pound New York white Cheddar cheese
> ¼ cup chopped white onions
> ¼ cup chopped jalapeño chilies, rinsed and seeded
> 3 dozen 8-inch flour tortillas
> Oil for deep frying

Grind cheese, onions, and chilies to a paste. Cut tortillas into quarters, place a teaspoonful of filling in the center of each quarter, fold ends to join and skewer with a toothpick. Deep-fry until golden brown. Remove toothpick before serving. Makes 12 dozen quesadillas.

NOTE: Picadillo or any highly seasoned seafood filling can be used in place of the cheese mixture for variety.

Seafood Empanadas

Empanadas are little Mexican turnovers and, of course, may have other fillings besides this recipe—meat, chicken, cheese with nuts, onions, and chopped chilies, or sweet fillings of mixed fruits and nuts. They can even be baked if you prefer. Place them on a baking sheet in a preheated 400° F. oven for about 5 minutes and serve at once.

> 2 cups all-purpose flour
> 1 teaspoon salt
> ⅔ cup lard
> 5 tablespoons ice water
> Filling (recipe follows)

Sift flour and salt together into a bowl. Cut half of the shortening into the flour mixture with a pastry blender until it is like fine corn meal. Cut the remaining half of the lard into the dough until it is about the size of peas. Add the ice water, blend lightly into the dough with a fork. Gather the dough into a ball, divide, and roll out a half at a time. Cut into 3-inch circles. Put about 2 teaspoons filling on one side of each circle of dough.

Dampen the edges and fold over into the shape of a crescent. Mark with tines of a fork to seal and fry in deep fat until golden brown. Drain on paper towels. Makes about 2 dozen empanadas.

FILLING FOR EMPANADAS

½ pound halibut, cod, or other lean white fish
2 tablespoons chopped onions
½ clove garlic, minced
2 tablespoons oil
Dash of white wine
2 teaspoons flour
½ teaspoon salt
¼ teaspoon pepper
1½ tablespoons fish or chicken stock
2 teaspoons minced jalapeño chili
2 teaspoons minced green onions
1 tablespoon crushed blanched almonds

Chop fish and sauté with onions and garlic in oil until about half cooked. Add a dash of wine, blend in flour, add salt and pepper, and stir; then stir in the stock. Remove from heat and add peppers, green onions, and almonds.

Nachos

This is the Mexican version of our melted cheese on crackers—only more lively with the addition of the chilies.

24 2-inch tortillas
¼ pound Cheddar cheese, grated
1 small can jalapeño chilies, rinsed, seeded, and sliced

Deep-fry the tortillas. This makes them tostadas. Sprinkle tostadas with grated cheese and place on cookie sheet. Slip under broiler until cheese melts. To serve, top with one slice of jalapeño chili.

Pine Nut Cheese Balls

2 8-ounce packages cream cheese
Cream to moisten
2 tablespoons finely chopped green pepper
4 teaspoons finely chopped pimiento
2 tablespoons finely chopped onions
1 teaspoon salt
Pine nuts

Soften the cheese just slightly with a little cream. Add the chopped vegetables and salt and blend well. Form into small balls about the size of a large marble and roll in pine nuts. Chill thoroughly before serving. Makes 3 dozen cheese balls.

Chili Cheese Balls

3 tablespoons chopped jalapeño chilies
½ pound grated Parmesan cheese
½ pound cream cheese
2 egg yolks
White bread crumbs

Mix ingredients together until they become smooth. Form the paste into marble-sized balls, ¾ to 1 inch in diameter. Spread white bread crumbs on a pastry board, then roll cheese balls in crumbs. Refrigerate first, then deep-fry in oil. Makes approximately 3 dozen cheese balls.

NOTE: You can use either the fresh jalapeños, preparing them as explained in the chili chapter, or the canned. If you use canned chilies, rinse them well, remove the seeds, and drain before chopping.

Señor Pico Guacamole

While we use guacamole primarily as a dip with tostadas or some kind of chips, it has many other delectable uses. For one, it makes a delicious molded salad (see Index for recipe). It also makes a wonderful dressing for a platter of sliced tomatoes, Bermuda onions, and cucumbers, and it can be added to hard-cooked egg yolks for distinguished stuffed eggs. Be sure and keep the avocado seed and bury it in the guacamole before you cover the dish with foil or plastic wrap to refrigerate until serving time. This prevents the mixture from turning dark.

> 2 medium-sized ripe avocados
> 1 large tomato
> 1 tablespoon chopped white onions
> ¼ cup French dressing
> 1 teaspoon finely chopped serrano chilies
> 1 dash Tabasco sauce
> Juice of ½ lime
> Salt and pepper to taste

Peel avocados, cut in half, and remove seeds. Place in a mixing bowl, break up avocado with a fork, and stir with wire whip until avocado is almost smooth but still retains some of its original consistency. Add all the other ingredients to the avocado and mix well. Serve with tostada chips. Makes 4 servings.

At Señor Pico's, we serve our guacamole in a "tostada basket," which is simply a large (6-inch) tortilla formed into the shape of a cup. This can be done by dropping the tortilla into hot oil for a few seconds. Place one wire strainer underneath the tortilla and a slightly smaller strainer on top of the tortilla. Press the strainers together to shape the tortilla into a cup as it crisps.

Chunky Guacamole

This recipe comes from a friend of a friend who makes it in quantities and freezes it to have on hand. Notice that the avocado in this guacamole is chopped into chunks and not mashed to a smooth consistency as in the Señor Pico recipe.

    4 avocados
    1 onion, finely diced
    1 unpeeled ripe tomato
    ½ cup roasted, peeled, and diced green chili*
    1 clove garlic, minced
    1 tablespoon olive oil
    1 tablespoon vinegar
    ¼ teaspoon powdered coriander
    Salt to taste

Peel and pit the avocados, chop the meat into small pieces, and place in a bowl. Add all the other ingredients and mix well to blend. Chill well before serving. Makes about 5 to 5½ cups guacamole.

* See chapter on chilies for preparation.

Refried Bean Dip

Refried beans make a wonderful cocktail dip. Leftover refried beans can be frozen and used for bean dips at a later date. Canned refried beans are available in most markets, and they are excellent for this purpose.

You can experiment with the seasonings of the bean dip with chopped jalapeño chilies instead of or in addition to the chili powder. Taste as you go so you don't get it too peppery hot.

1 can refried beans
½ teaspoon chili powder
3 dashes Tabasco sauce
2 tablespoons finely chopped onions
2 heaping tablespoons sour cream
Salt to taste

Mix ingredients well in a bowl and refrigerate at least an hour before serving. Serve with tostadas or corn chips.

Chile con Queso—No. 1
Chili with Cheese

One of my favorite dips to accompany cocktails is chile con queso—a cheese and chili mixture that you can keep warm in a fondue pot. For dipping, use tostadas, which are simply deep-fried triangles of tortillas. You can make your own or use packaged tortilla chips, which are available in most grocery stores.

3 cups light cream or half-and-half
¼ pound New York white Cheddar cheese, grated
½ pound Monterey Jack cheese, grated
2 tablespoons minced onions
1 small clove garlic, minced
1 tablespoon butter
6 tablespoons white wine
¼ cup cornstarch mixed with
¼ cup cold water

¼ cup chopped canned jalapeño chilies, rinsed and seeded
1 teaspoon monosodium glutamate
Salt and white pepper to taste

In the upper half of a double boiler, heat the cream, add the grated cheese, and set over low heat to melt. In a saucepan, sauté the onions and garlic in the butter until onions are transparent. Add half of the wine to the garlic and onions, swish it around in the pan, and pour into the cheese mixture, stirring well. (Meanwhile, put hot water in bottom of double boiler and set over heat.) Thicken the cheese mixture with the cornstarch mixed to a paste with the water, stirring constantly. Add chopped chilies, seasonings, and the other half of the wine and mix thoroughly. Set over hot water until ready to use. Transfer to fondue pot and serve with tostada chips. Makes about 4½ cups dip.

Chile con Queso—No. 2

This version of chile con queso comes from a friend of mine who entertains a good deal, so she makes this recipe in large quantities and stores it in her freezer for a variety of interesting uses. She tells me it keeps beautifully and can be reheated in a double boiler in a very short time.

½ pound Cheddar cheese
½ pound Monterey Jack cheese
½ cup heavy cream or evaporated milk
1 cup diced, roasted, and peeled green chilies*
1 teaspoon orégano
½ teaspoon powdered cumin
2 cups tomato juice
2 cloves garlic, crushed
Salt to taste

Cut up the cheeses into fairly small pieces and heat with the cream in the top of a double boiler until cheese is melted. Add the remaining ingredients, stir well to blend flavors, and continue to heat and stir until the mixture is smooth. Transfer to a fondue pot to keep warm and serve as a cocktail dip with tostadas or packaged tortilla chips. If you plan to store all or any in the freezer, be sure to first let the mixture cool before freezing. Makes about 4½ cups chile con queso dip.

Here are some of the other ways my friend uses her chile con queso:

As a sauce for cooked fresh green beans to accompany enchiladas or other Mexican dishes.

As a topping for crêpes (thin pancakes) rolled around little pig sausages. Makes a great dish for brunch.

As a topping for a crisp-fried tortilla, placed on a shallow pan and run under the broiler until brown and bubbly hot.

* See chapter on chilies for preparation.

Chili Almonds

These are great for nibbling with cocktails.

1 stick butter
1 large clove garlic, slightly crushed
1 tablespoon chili powder
1 pound shelled but unblanched almonds
Salt to taste

In a large, heavy skillet, heat the butter and sauté the clove of garlic until limp; discard the clove. Mix in the chili powder until thoroughly blended; then add the almonds and stir constantly over medium heat until the nuts are well coated and slightly browned. Sprinkle with salt and let cool before serving.

Chiles
[Chilies]

There is probably more misunderstanding about chilies than any other vegetable grown, in spite of the fact that they are all members of the genus Capsicum, the same family that produces the dependably mild green bell pepper, sweet red pepper, and pimiento.

The confusion is understandable when you consider that, in Mexico alone, there are over sixty varieties of chilies, according to some botanists. According to others, the count is closer to ninety. To add to the problem, chilies cross-pollinate with the greatest of ease and the same plant will often produce both hot and mild pods. On top of all this, some of the fresh chilies are called by different names in different groceries and canned chilies are not always consistently labeled. As you can see, it pays to taste before you add chilies too generously to the dish you are cooking.

One thing you can be sure of is that fresh chilies are an exceptionally rich source of Vitamins A and C. The Vitamin C is lost in the dried red chilies, but canned and frozen chilies retain about two-thirds of their vitamin content. And in all cases, chilies are one of the best known of all natural aids to digestion.

In typical Mexican cooking, the green chilies—which are usually hotter than the red—are used fresh; and the red chilies are used dried. For the most part, my recipes call for canned chilies because they're quicker and easier and also because the fresh—and even the dried—varieties are not always available outside of California and the Southwest.

Anyway, here is a list to acquaint you with the chilies called for in this cookbook, the directions for preparing them, and the substitutions you can use.

THE FRESH GREEN CHILIES

California Green Chili

This is the mildest of the lot, about 5 to 8 inches long, tapering to a point. When canned, it is usually labeled "Green Chilies" or sometimes just "Whole Chilies."

Poblano

This is the chili used for chiles rellenos (stuffed chilies). It resembles the green bell pepper in shape, which, by the way, makes an adequate substitution for it. The poblano is usually mild, with only a faint trace of heat.

Jalapeño

This one packs quite a lot of heat in its small pod, which

is only about 2½ inches long. While it is called a green chili, it will sometimes be yellow in color.

Serrano

Proceed with caution when you use this tiny pod. It's only about 1 to 1½ inches long, but it's full of fire. Some markets carry a mixture of small fresh green and red chilies simply called hot peppers. These chilies vary from 1 to 3 inches in length and can be used in place of the serranos.

THE DRIED RED CHILIES

Ancho

This one is on the mild side and rather sweet in flavor with only a faint trace of heat. The ancho is sort of flat and roundish, about 3 to 4 inches in diameter.

Mulato

This one has a larger, more tapering pod than the ancho chili and is more brownish than red in color. However, the flavor is much like the ancho, and the two can be interchangeable in recipes.

Pasilla

Hot and pungent, this chocolate-brown colored chili is thin and about 7 inches long.

Chipotle

This chili is not as large as the mulato, but it is extremely hot.

HOW TO PREPARE FRESH CHILIES

A word of warning before you handle any chilies. Once your fingers touch the seeds, where most of the fire is contained, or even the oil in the flesh of the pod, *don't rub your eyes* without first scrubbing your hands thoroughly with soap and water. Otherwise, you'll get one helluva painful sting.

There are several ways the Mexicans peel and deseed their fresh chilies, but the following method is, I think, the quickest and easiest.

First, rinse the chilies in cold water and wipe them dry with paper towels. Lay them close together on a foil-covered cookie sheet or oven rack. Preheat your broiler and place the rack about 3 inches under the flame so that the tops of the chilies are about 1 inch below the heat. Leave the broiler door open so that you can watch closely, and turn the chilies frequently (metal tongs are a good tool) until they are lightly browned and blistered all over. Remove each one as it is done and place it in a brown paper bag or a plastic film bag. Keep the bag closed so that the chilies will steam as they cool and be easier to peel. Cooling takes about 5 to 10 minutes. Or you can plunge the blistered chilies into a bowl of ice water—a good idea when you are planning to stuff them for chiles rellenos and want to keep them a little crisper. If you want your chilies less hot in flavor, add some salt to the water and let them soak for about an hour.

As soon as the chilies are cool, peel off the skin with a sharp paring knife. It usually comes off easily in large patches, but it's better to leave a small piece of skin on than to tear the chili if you're planning to stuff it.

To prepare the peeled chilies for stuffing, cut a slit down one side to within about ¼ inch of the stem. Spoon out the seeds and the veins (ribs). The stem should be left on as a handle for dipping the stuffed chilies into the batter.

If the chilies are going to be cut up for a recipe, simply cut off the stem, any hard core at the top, and remove the seeds by rinsing them out with cold water.

51

Fresh chilies can be prepared a day ahead and refrigerated in plastic wrap. Or they can be kept frozen for many months at 0 degrees.

HOW TO PREPARE DRIED CHILIES

Wash the chilies in cold water and, holding them under the running water, pull out the stem; cut or break the chilies in half and remove the seeds and veins. Then tear the chilies into small pieces; place in a bowl and cover with boiling water. Let soak for 40 minutes to an hour before using. The water in which they have soaked can be used as part of the liquid in the recipe.

HOW TO PREPARE CANNED CHILIES

This is very easy. You simply rinse the chilies very thoroughly to rid them of any flavor of the brine in which they were preserved. If you are using the canned California green chilies for stuffing, follow the same directions as for the fresh. If you are using them for other purposes, just remove the stems, the veins and the seeds.

In buying canned chilies, be careful not to get the pickled ones (*en escabeche*) unless specified in a recipe, as the pickling cannot be rinsed away and will really louse up the flavor of the dish.

SUBSTITUTIONS

Fresh green bell peppers, canned poblano or canned California green chilies may be substituted for fresh poblano chilies in the chiles rellenos recipes.

Cayenne pepper can be substituted for chili pequín powder, which is made from a very hot dried chili. One tablespoon of chili powder may be substituted for one fresh or dried chili. Many Mexican cooks make a chili paste for this substitution by mixing the chili powder with flour and water. The proportions are 1 tablespoon chili powder, 1 teaspoon flour, and 2 tablespoons cold water. When adding this paste to the cooking, it should reach a boil to effect the proper seasoning.

NOTE: The chili powder we normally buy from our supermarket spice shelves is actually a blend of several spices and herbs. While this will suffice, you can buy powdered ancho, mulato, or pasilla powder in Mexican groceries if you want the pure chili flavor when called for in a recipe.

Señor Pico Chiles Rellenos con Queso
Chilies Stuffed with Cheese

In Mexico, chiles rellenos, or stuffed chili peppers, are made with fresh poblano chilies. If you can't find canned poblano chilies in a Mexican grocery store, you can substitute fresh green bell peppers or canned California green chilies.

Standard procedure for chiles rellenos is to prepare the chilies as directed in this chapter, stuff them, dredge them with flour, dip in batter, and deep-fry in oil. After eating hundreds of chiles rellenos from here to Mexico, I decided that there must be a better way to do it, so we experimented, and now we bake our chiles rellenos at Señor Pico. However, the restaurant process requires special equipment and is too complicated for home use, but you can try this method, using individual baking dishes for each stuffed chili.

        6 canned poblano chilies
        6 2-inch strips Monterey Jack cheese, about ½ inch thick
        6 2-inch strips New York Cheddar cheese, about ½ inch
            thick
        Flour

1 cup egg whites (about 8)
½ cup egg yolks (about 6)
4 tablespoons melted butter
Señor Pico Sauce for Chiles Rellenos (recipe follows)

Preheat oven to 375° F. Prepare chilies as directed in this chapter and drain thoroughly. Put a piece of Jack cheese and a piece of Cheddar in each pod. Dust the pods with flour.

Beat egg whites until stiff. Beat egg yolks and then combine the two. Just before you are ready to coat the stuffed peppers, add melted butter to egg mixture. Be sure it is just melted and not hot. Meanwhile, oil 6 individual baking dishes. Pour a thick coating of batter into the baking dishes; place each stuffed pepper in a baking dish of batter, then spoon the rest of the batter on top. Bake for 15 minutes. Makes 6 servings.

To serve, remove chiles rellenos from baking dish to plate and top with Señor Pico Sauce for Chiles Rellenos. Serve with an enchilada or tamale (or both) and refried beans and rice.

SEÑOR PICO SAUCE FOR CHILES RELLENOS

½ cup chopped onions
1 clove garlic, minced
1 tablespoon oil
2 tablespoons tomato paste
1 cup chopped peeled tomatoes
1 can chicken broth (1⅓ cups)
1 teaspoon sugar
½ teaspoon salt
1 teaspoon vinegar
1 tablespoon flour

Sauté onions and garlic in the oil until onions are transparent; add tomato paste and chopped tomatoes and let simmer for a few minutes. Add broth, sugar, salt, and vinegar. Let simmer until tomatoes have disintegrated, then whirl in electric blender to a smooth purée. Reheat and thicken lightly with flour mixed with 1 or 2 tablespoons cold water. Continue cooking, stirring frequently, until sauce comes to a boil. Serve over chiles rellenos. Makes about 3 cups sauce.

Mexican Chiles Rellenos

In case you prefer to deep-fry your chiles rellenos, here is a Mexican recipe with a meat filling.

PREPARATION OF CHILIES FOR MEXICAN CHILES RELLENOS

4 eggs, separated
12 canned poblano chilies
½ cup flour
Oil for frying

Beat egg whites until stiff; beat egg yolks and combine the two. Stuff poblanos with meat filling (see following recipe). Cover them well with flour, and then roll in egg batter and fry in deep fat at 375° F. until golden brown. Remove, drain on paper towels, and place in sauce (see recipe following the meat filling). Boil up and serve. Makes 6 servings of 2 chilies each.

FILLING FOR MEXICAN CHILES RELLENOS

2 onions, chopped
2 tablespoons oil
½ pound ground beef
½ pound ground pork
1 cup chopped peeled tomatoes
1 teaspoon salt
½ teaspoon pepper
½ teaspoon ground cinnamon
½ teaspoon chopped candied citron

2 tablespoons vinegar
2 tablespoons chopped blanched almonds
2 tablespoons chopped pine nuts

Sauté onions in oil until transparent, then add ground meat. Stir until meat is crumbly and cooked, then add chopped tomatoes, seasonings, citron, vinegar, and nuts. Let simmer over low heat until thick. Makes filling for 6 servings.

SAUCE FOR MEXICAN CHILES RELLENOS

1 onion, chopped
1 tablespoon oil
1½ pounds chopped peeled tomatoes
1 piece stick cinnamon
1 cup beef stock or consommé
1 teaspoon salt
¼ teaspoon pepper
3 tablespoons chopped parsley

Sauté onion in oil until transparent, add chopped tomatoes and cinnamon and let simmer until tomatoes are mushy. Remove cinnamon and purée the mixture in an electric blender. Reheat, add beef stock, salt, and pepper. Simmer until thickened. Add fried chilies, boil up once and serve. Garnish with chopped parsley. Makes about 4 cups sauce.

Chiles Rellenos con Frijoles Refritos
Stuffed Chilies with Refried Beans

6 canned poblano chilies
2 tablespoons finely chopped onions
1 tablespoon oil
2 tablespoons tomato paste
½ teaspoon orégano

2 cups refried beans
3 dashes Tabasco sauce
Salt and pepper to taste
Flour
Egg batter*
½ cup sour cream
½ cup grated Cheddar cheese

Prepare the chilies for stuffing as directed in this chapter and set aside. Sauté the chopped onions in the oil until limp; add tomato paste and orégano and let cook for a few seconds, then add beans and seasonings. Blend and let cook for a few minutes. Stuff chilies with bean mixture, then dust well with flour and roll in egg batter. Deep-fry in oil until golden brown. Remove and drain on paper towels. Arrange in greased baking dish. Cover with sour cream and grated cheese. Bake in a preheated 350° F. oven until lightly browned. Makes 6 servings.

* To prepare egg batter, see directions in recipe for Señor Pico Chiles Rellenos.

Chile con Elote
Chili and Corn Casserole

1 4-ounce can California green chilies
2 cups drained canned whole kernel corn, reserving liquid drained from can
½ cup melted butter
2 eggs, beaten
½ cup yellow corn meal
½ teaspoon salt
1 cup sour cream
¼ pound Monterey Jack cheese, diced
¼ pound Cheddar cheese, diced

Prepare the chilies as directed in this chapter, drain them, chop them coarsely, and place in a mixing bowl. Whirl the corn in an electric blender with 2 or 3 tablespoons of reserved corn liquid for a few seconds; then add to the chilies in mixing bowl. Add the butter, eggs, corn meal, salt, sour cream, and diced cheese and mix all thoroughly. Pour the mixture into a buttered casserole and bake in a preheated 350° F. oven for 45 minutes to an hour, or until golden brown and firm to the touch. Makes 6 to 8 servings.

Chile con Queso y Arroz
Chilies and Cheese with Rice

> 1 4-ounce can California green chilies
> 1 pint sour cream
> 3 cups cooked rice
> 1 teaspoon orégano
> Salt and pepper to taste
> 2 cups (½ pound) grated Cheddar cheese
> Chopped chives
> Paprika

Prepare the chilies as directed in this chapter and chop them coarsely; then mix them thoroughly into the sour cream. Season the rice with the orégano, salt and pepper to taste. In a well-buttered casserole, alternate layers of rice, layers of chilies and sour cream, and layers of cheese (saving a small amount of cheese). End with a layer of rice. Bake, covered, in a preheated 350° F. oven for about 20 minutes. Uncover, sprinkle the top with the reserved cheese, and bake for another 10 minutes or until cheese is bubbly. Garnish with chopped chives and a sprinkling of paprika. Makes 6 servings.

Salsas
[Sauces]

There's hardly a Mexican dish from soup to rice to beans to tortillas—you name it—that doesn't call for a sauce, either as an ingredient in the cooking, a topping, or served separately at the table.

When the sauce is an integral part of the dish or a traditional accompaniment to it, you'll find the recipe given with that specific dish wherever it appears in this book.

This chapter is devoted to those good sauces that can be served separately with a number of different foods, as in the case of *salsa cruda*, the uncooked tomato sauce that comes to the table freshly made with almost every Mexican meal. Guacamole is another standard Mexican table sauce, but since it is served more often in the States as a cocktail dip, you'll find it listed under Antojitos (Appetizers).

Canned enchilada sauces and Spanish red chili sauces are quite similar and are usually available in our supermarkets, and there are more to be found in Mexican grocery stores. These are mighty handy when you're in a hurry, and if you find them a little too hot for your taste, you can easily temper the flavor by mixing them with a plain tomato sauce.

Salsa Cruda—No. 1
Uncooked Tomato Sauce

A bowl of this fresh seasoned tomato sauce is customarily served with most Mexican meals, even though each family may vary the seasonings to their own taste from mild to very hot.

> 2 large tomatoes, chopped
> 3 canned California green chilies, rinsed, seeded, and chopped
> 1 large onion, finely chopped
> 1 tablespoon chopped parsley
> 1 teaspoon minced garlic
> 1 teaspoon salt
> ½ teaspoon pepper
> Juice of 1 lemon
> 1 tablespoon olive oil (optional)

Combine all ingredients and mix thoroughly; chill before serving. Salsa cruda will keep well for several days if refrigerated in a covered container. Makes about 3 cups.

Salsa Cruda—No. 2

> 3 medium-sized ripe tomatoes
> ½ cup finely chopped onions

1 tablespoon chopped parsley
2 fresh or canned serrano chilies, minced
Salt, pepper, and sugar to taste

Peel and chop tomatoes; combine with onions, parsley, and serrano chilies. Season to taste and chill well before serving. Makes about 2 cups sauce.

Salsa Verde
Uncooked Green Sauce

3 fresh or canned serrano chilies, chopped
1 12-ounce can Mexican green tomatoes, drained and chopped
1 onion, finely chopped
1 clove garlic, minced
1 tablespoon chopped parsley
1 teaspoon salt
½ teaspoon pepper
Juice of 1 lemon

If using fresh chilies, prepare according to directions in the chili chapter. If using canned chilies, rinse, seed, and drain them before chopping. Combine all ingredients and mix thoroughly to blend flavors. Makes about 1½ cups.

Texas-Mex Salsa Verde
Green Sauce

This is a favorite sauce for enchiladas with some of my Texas friends, but it also goes well with fish or chicken.

2 10-ounce packages frozen peas, thawed
¼ cup chopped onions

½ teaspoon chopped garlic
1 No. 2½ can Ortega green chilies, rinsed, seeded, and
 drained
2 cans cream of mushroom soup
¼ to ½ cup chicken broth
Salt and pepper to taste

Purée peas, onions, garlic and chilies in blender. Combine with cream of mushroom soup and mix thoroughly. Use chicken broth to thin sauce; place in pan and simmer for 15 minutes. Season to taste. Makes approximately 2 quarts.

Texas-Mex Tomato Table Sauce

If you're throwing a big shindig, here's a big recipe for plenty of sauce to liven things up.

10 small fresh green chilies, minced
1 medium-sized white onion, very finely chopped
2 cloves garlic, minced
1 tablespoon chopped Chinese parsley
10 peeled tomatoes, chopped
2 tablespoons vinegar
2 tablespoons olive oil
½ teaspoon Tabasco sauce
Salt to taste

Prepare chilies according to direction in the chili chapter. Combine chilies, onion, garlic, and Chinese parsley. Add tomatoes and remaining ingredients. Mix well and store in covered glass containers in refrigerator until needed. Makes about 2½ to 3 quarts sauce, depending on size of tomatoes.

Salsa Ranchera
Ranch Style Sauce

> 1 clove garlic, minced
> 1 tablespoon oil
> 1 small green fresh or canned chili, chopped
> 1 No. 300 can (1¾ cups) Spanish-style tomato sauce
> Salt and pepper to taste

Sauté garlic in oil and add chopped chili. Add tomato sauce and let simmer a few minutes to blend flavors. Season with salt and pepper.

If using a fresh chili, prepare according to directions in the chili chapter. If using a canned chili, rinse, seed, and drain it before chopping. Makes about 2 cups sauce.

Salsa Borracha
Drunken Sauce

This is a good sauce to serve over pork, beef, beans, or eggs.

> ¼ pound fresh yellow chilies
> 2 cups water
> 1 No. 2½ can tomatoes, chopped
> 1 clove garlic, finely chopped
> 1 white onion, chopped
> 4 to 6 sprigs Chinese parsley, chopped
> 1 tablespoon oil
> 1½ tablespoons vinegar
> ¾ cup beer
> 1 tablespoon salt
> ½ teaspoon pepper
> ½ teaspoon orégano

½ teaspoon powdered cumin
3 to 4 green onions, chopped

Boil chilies in water until stems can be easily removed; drain, reserving the liquid. Remove stems and seeds; chop chilies. Combine all ingredients and mix well. If mixture is too thick, thin with some of the reserved liquid from cooking the chilies. Heat to boiling before serving. Makes about 3 cups.

Salsa Guadalajara
Sauce Guadalajara Style

I had this sauce on an enchilada in Guadalajara and liked it so much I wheedled the recipe out of the cook. It would be just as good on tortillas and tacos, too.

1 large onion, peeled and chopped
1 clove garlic, peeled and minced
1 large tomato, peeled and chopped
1 stick butter
2 cups buttermilk
¼ cup sour cream
Salt and pepper to taste
2 tablespoons chopped Chinese parsley
4 black pitted olives, sliced

Sauté onion, garlic, and tomato in the butter; add buttermilk and sour cream. Let cook, stirring constantly, just to boiling point. Reduce heat at once; season with salt and pepper to taste. Remove from stove and stir in the parsley and olives. Serve while hot. Makes about 3½ cups sauce.

Señor Pico Salsa de Pipián
Señor Pico Pumpkin Seed Sauce

At Señor Pico, we serve this pumpkin seed sauce with boiled corned tongue and chicken breasts.

½ pound pumpkin seeds, shelled
1½ cups chicken stock
½ pound dried California chilies
1 cup water
1 clove garlic, minced
Salt to taste
½ cup sour cream
½ cup seedless raisins

Soak pumpkin seeds in water for 24 hours. Drain and put into blender with 1 cup of the chicken stock; purée to a smooth paste. Remove from blender and set aside. Remove stems and seeds from chilies. Place in 1 cup water and bring to a boil. Drain and put into blender with the remaining ½ cup chicken stock; blend until puréed. Strain chili purée into a pan; bring to a boil. Remove from heat; add the puréed pumpkin seeds, garlic, and salt. Stir to make a smooth heavy sauce. (Consistency should be like that of heavy cream.) Add sour cream and raisins. Makes about 3 cups.

Salsa de Pipián—No. 2
Pumpkin Seed Sauce

Here's another good pumpkin seed sauce that goes great with seafood and also cocktail meatballs. Or, you can add it to partially cooked chicken or meat and let the dish finish cooking in the sauce.

This recipe calls for *pepitas*, which are already-shelled

pumpkin seeds, where the kernels have been toasted and flavored. Pepitas are available, usually in jars, in many supermarkets.

¾ cup Mexican pepitas
2 tablespoons peanut butter
2 cloves garlic, chopped
2 tablespoons pasilla chili powder
1 small white onion, chopped
1½ cups tomato juice
2 tablespoons masa harina or wheat flour
⅔ cup chicken broth

Put all ingredients, except the chicken broth, into a blender and blend until smooth. Add the puréed mixture to the chicken broth in a saucepan; heat and simmer for about 10 minutes, stirring occasionally, to blend flavors. Serve hot. Makes about 2½ cups sauce.

Sopas
(Soups)

Dinnertime in Mexico is anytime from early to midafternoon, and this main meal—the *comida*—had better start with soup or Mama is going to hear it from Papa. So, much like the *pot au feu* of France, the Mexican housewife has a soup pot on the stove every day to provide homemade stock as the basis for all kinds of interesting soups.

Few of our American women have this kind of time on their hands. So even though these recipes specify chicken or beef stock, you can simply substitute a can of chicken or beef broth. If you use bouillon cubes instead of the canned broths, they'll be saltier, so taste as you proceed and cut down on the salting of the soup if necessary.

Since Mexicans take their soup so seriously, you can bet your sweet life they turn out some dandies. I've had to omit some good ones, such as squash blossom soup, for lack of ingredients available in the States, but you'll find plenty of treats in this chapter for the soup lovers in your family.

Señor Pico Gazpacho
Cold Mexican Soup

> 2 cloves garlic, cut
> 5 tomatoes, peeled, seeded, and finely chopped
> 3 cucumbers, peeled, seeded, and finely chopped
> 1 cup minced green bell pepper
> 3 stalks celery, diced
> ½ cup finely chopped onions
> 2 to 2½ cups tomato juice
> ⅓ cup olive oil
> ½ cup lemon juice
> 1 quart cold water (approximately)
> 1 teaspoon Tabasco or to taste
> Salt and pepper to taste
> Chopped parsley or sour cream for garnish

Rub glass or stainless steel bowl with garlic and discard cloves. Add the tomatoes, cucumbers, minced green pepper, diced celery, and onions. Over this pour the tomato juice, olive oil, and lemon juice. Add cold water until desired consistency. Season with Tabasco and salt and pepper to taste. Chill. Serve in individual chilled bowls with 2 ice cubes in each. Garnish with parsley or sour cream. Makes 6 to 8 servings.

Gazpacho—No. 2

Here is another version of Mexico's famous cold, spicy soup.

3 tablespoons water
4 3-inch peelings of cucumber rind
1 small onion, chopped
½ green pepper, seeded and chopped
1 clove garlic, cut up
1 teaspoon salt, or to taste
6 slices white bread, trimmed of crusts
¼ cup water
¼ cup wine vinegar
¼ cup salad oil
1 teaspoon monosodium glutamate
4 large tomatoes, peeled, seeded, and chopped
6 cups thick tomato juice
Garnishes

Place the water in blender; add the cucumber peelings, onion, green pepper, garlic, and salt. Blend until smoothly puréed. Soak the bread slices in a mixture of the water, vinegar, oil, monosodium glutamate, and chopped tomatoes; add to mixture in blender and blend until smooth. Add the vegetable purée to the tomato juice, blending it well, and chill until very cold. Serve in chilled bowls and pass a garnish plate with mounds of finely chopped onion, celery, green pepper, and croutons that have been sautéed in butter. Makes about 9½ cups.

Sopa de Pipino Frío
Cold Cucumber Soup

Here is another cold soup of Mexico and one you'll find really beats the heat when served as a light lunch or with hot weather meals.

2 tablespoons butter
3 tablespoons flour
1 5½-ounce can evaporated milk
1 very large or 2 small cucumbers, peeled and diced
1 quart water
Salt and pepper to taste
2 drops green food coloring
¼ cup minced parsley
½ cup sour cream

Melt the butter in a large saucepan and stir in the flour to make a thick paste. Cook very gently for several minutes over low heat until golden, taking care not to scorch. Add the milk, a little at a time, stirring constantly, until mixture is thickened and smooth; remove from heat. Place cucumbers in blender with 3 tablespoons of the water and blend until smooth. Slowly add the cucumber mixture and the rest of the water to the cooked sauce, stirring to blend thoroughly. Bring mixture just to a boil, reduce heat, and simmer for 20 minutes. Let cool. Add salt and pepper to taste and mix in the coloring; then the parsley and the sour cream. Serve very cold in chilled soup cups. Makes 6 to 8 servings.

Sopa de Camarón
Shrimp Soup

½ pound shrimp in their shells
1½ quarts chicken stock
1 teaspoon allspice
1 tablespoon butter
1 clove garlic
1 10½-ounce can condensed tomato soup
⅛ teaspoon chili powder
Salt and pepper to taste

Shell the shrimp, devein the meat, wash, and set aside. Thoroughly wash the shells and boil them in the chicken stock, adding the allspice.

Meanwhile, in a large saucepan, heat the butter and gently sauté the garlic until limp. Discard the garlic and add the tomato soup and the cleaned shrimp. Strain the stock in which the shells were boiled and add to the tomato-shrimp mixture. Simmer slowly for 20 minutes. Add the chili powder and salt and pepper to taste. Makes 6 servings.

Sopa de Camaron Sinaloense
Shrimp Soup Sinaloa Style

    1 pound unshelled raw shrimp
    2 quarts water
    2 teaspoons salt
    1 onion, peeled and cut in half
    1 teaspoon chili pequín powder
    4 tablespoons masa harina
    ½ cup white wine
    ½ cup sour cream

Thoroughly wash the shrimp and boil them for about 15 to 20 minutes in the water with the salt and onion. Discard the onion and remove the shrimp to peel and devein. Skim the foam from the surface of the broth.

Mix the chili powder with the masa harina; dilute the mixture by stirring some of the broth into it; then return the mixture to the broth. Let simmer, stirring frequently, until the soup has thickened a little; then add the wine and blend it in. Just before serving, slowly stir in the sour cream. Serve the soup with 3 or 4 whole peeled shrimp in each plate. Makes 6 servings.

Sopa de Pescado Veracruz
Veracruz Fish Soup

FISH STOCK

2 pounds fish heads, tails, and bones, washed
4 quarts cold water
1 bay leaf
½ teaspoon orégano
1 cup chopped onions
1 cup chopped celery
2 teaspoons salt
½ teaspoon pepper
2 teaspoons monosodium glutamate
1 cup white wine

Place fish heads, tails, and bones in a soup kettle. Add water and remaining ingredients except wine. Bring to a boil. Add wine and continue to cook, uncovered, at a moderate boil for about 45 minutes. Discard bones. Lay a cloth in a colander over another pot and strain, mashing onions and celery to a dry pulp.

FINISHED SOUP

Strained soup stock (about 8 to 9 cups)
1 cup peeled and chopped tomatoes
2 tablespoons flour
2 cups diced raw halibut, cod, or other white fish
4 tablespoons chopped celery leaves
Salt and pepper to taste

Bring fish stock to a boil; add chopped tomatoes and thicken slightly with flour mixed with a little cold water. Add the diced fish and celery leaves. Bring to a boil and simmer for

20 minutes, or until fish is done. Correct seasonings. Makes about 11 cups.

Caldo de Arroz con Pollo
Chicken Rice Soup

>   2 quarts chicken stock
>   ½ cup raw white rice
>   2 cups canned or fresh chopped tomatoes
>   3 tablespoons finely chopped onions
>   1 clove garlic, pressed
>   2 tablespoons finely chopped parsley
>   Salt and pepper to taste
>   4 cooked chicken livers, chopped
>   4 chicken gizzards, chopped
>   2 hard-cooked eggs, finely chopped for garnish

Bring stock to a boil and stir in the rice. When stock returns to a boil, add the tomatoes, onions, garlic, parsley, salt and pepper, and let simmer for 15 minutes. Add the chopped giblets and continue simmering for about 30 minutes or until rice is done. Sprinkle each serving with a garnish of the finely chopped hard-cooked eggs. Makes 8 servings.

Sopa de Pollo con Jericalla
Chicken Soup with Custard Garnish

>   4 eggs, lightly beaten
>   8 cups well-seasoned chicken stock
>   1 teaspoon cornstarch
>   Pinch of nutmeg
>   Salt and white pepper to taste
>   ½ cup dry sherry

To make the custard, place the beaten eggs in the top of a double boiler over hot (not boiling) water. Gradually stir in 1 cup of the cool chicken stock and the cornstarch, stirring constantly; then blend in the nutmeg and salt and pepper to taste. Cover and cook over hot water (do not let it heat above simmering) for about 20 minutes or as long as it takes for custard to set. Remove from heat and let thoroughly cool. Just before serving, heat the soup and add the sherry. Cut the custard into small squares, the size of croutons, and serve as a garnish with the soup. Makes 8 servings.

Sopa de Albóndiga
Meatball Soup

This soup, made with meatballs, is great for lunch with a green salad, French bread, and plenty of red wine.

SOUP

½ cup finely chopped onions
1 clove garlic, minced
2 tablespoons oil
1 teaspoon chili powder
⅔ cup peeled, chopped tomatoes
2 quarts beef consommé
Albondiguitas (recipe follows)

Sauté onions and garlic in oil until limp and transparent. Add chili powder and chopped tomatoes and let cook for a few more minutes, stirring to blend flavors. Add the consommé and bring to a boil. Reduce heat and let simmer while you prepare the little albóndigas.

ALBONDIGUITAS (LITTLE MEATBALLS)

½ pound ground beef
½ pound ground pork
½ cup cooked rice
1 tablespoon cornstarch
⅛ teaspoon garlic powder
¼ teaspoon orégano
1 teaspoon salt
¼ teaspoon pepper
1 egg, slightly beaten
¼ cup chopped Chinese parsley

Combine meat and rice in mixing bowl. Add cornstarch, seasonings, and egg. Mix thoroughly by hand and shape into balls about the size of a walnut. Bring broth to a boil; drop meatballs into boiling broth. Cover and cook for about 30 minutes. Pour the soup into a tureen and ladle into individual bowls, putting several meatballs into each bowl. Sprinkle each portion with a little chopped parsley. Makes 6 to 8 servings.

Sopa Azteca
Aztec Soup

½ cup chopped onions
½ cup chopped okra
4 tablespoons butter
4 tablespoons chopped celery leaves
2 teaspoons crushed basil leaves
3 quarts chicken stock
1 tablespoon tomato paste
Salt and pepper to taste
½ cup sherry
½ cup cooked, diced calf brains

Tostada slices
Diced avocado
Pasilla chili powder

Sauté onions and okra in butter until onions are limp but not browned. Stir in celery leaves and basil until blended; then add chicken stock mixed with the tomato paste. Add salt and pepper and bring to a boil. Reduce heat and let simmer for 30 minutes. Add sherry and calf brains and let simmer for a few minutes to heat the brains before serving. Correct seasonings and ladle soup into bowls over 1 tablespoon tostada slices and 1 tablespoon diced avocado. Sprinkle lightly with chili powder. Makes about 14 cups of soup.

Sopa de Calabaza
Squash Soup

1 pound zucchini or summer squash, cut into small
    chunks
1 large onion, chopped
6 cups beef stock
1 egg yolk
½ cup light cream
Salt and pepper to taste

Cook the squash and the onion in the stock until tender and soft. Press through a sieve and return the sieved mixture to the broth; keep hot. Beat the egg yolk with the cream. Slowly stir a ladleful of the soup into the egg mixture; then carefully whisk the egg mixture into the soup. Add salt and pepper to taste. Heat through but do not allow to boil. Makes 6 servings.

Crema de Aguacates
Cream of Avocado Soup

>   2 tablespoons butter
>   2 tablespoons flour
>   1 quart milk, heated
>   1 very ripe, large avocado
>   Lemon juice
>   1 cup light cream
>   Salt and pepper to taste
>   Chili powder to taste
>   Crisp tostadas
>   1 firm avocado for garnish

In a large pan, melt the butter, mix in the flour, and stir until smooth. Cook for a few minutes, stirring constantly, but do not allow to brown. Add hot milk a little at a time, stirring constantly, and cook over low heat until sauce begins to thicken slightly. Peel and mash the very ripe avocado with a little lemon juice to prevent its getting dark. Add the avocado pulp to the white sauce, together with the cream. Season well and serve very hot, garnished with the tostadas and the other avocado, peeled and diced. Makes 6 servings.

Sopa de Lentejas
Lentil Soup

A good hearty soup for nippy weather and one you can make ahead, for it keeps well in the freezer.

>   1 cup dried lentils
>   1 teaspoon salt
>   2 or 3 peppercorns
>   ½ bay leaf

½ cup diced carrots
½ cup chopped celery tops
1 quart beef stock
4 slices bacon, cut into squares
1 medium onion, chopped
½ cup tomato purée

Soak lentils overnight in water to cover. Next day, drain the lentils and add them with the salt, peppercorns, bay leaf, carrots, and celery tops to the stock to simmer. Fry the bacon pieces lightly; remove from pan. In 2 tablespoons of the bacon fat, lightly sauté the onion, add the tomato purée, and simmer for 10 minutes. Add the tomato-onion mixture with the bacon pieces to the soup kettle and simmer for about an hour or until lentils are tender. Makes 6 servings.

Sopa de Frijol Negro
Black Bean Soup

1 cup dried black beans
2 quarts cold water
4 strips bacon or salt pork, cut into pieces
1 medium onion, chopped
1 clove garlic, chopped
1 large tomato, peeled and chopped
¼ teaspoon orégano
1 teaspoon chili powder
2 teaspoons salt or more to taste
½ cup dry sherry
6 slices lime or lemon

Wash beans thoroughly and soak for 8 hours or overnight. Drain them and place them in a soup kettle with 2 quarts water. Cover and simmer gently for about 5 hours (the longer, the better with these beans). In a skillet, render the bacon or salt pork and gently sauté the onion and garlic (adding oil, if necessary, to equal 4 tablespoons fat). When the onion is limp and golden, stir in the chopped tomato, orégano, chili powder, and salt. Stir this mixture into the beans and simmer, covered, for another 30 minutes or more (by this time the beans should be very tender). Press the beans through a sieve or purée them in a blender; then return them to the soup to reheat. When hot, stir in the sherry and serve each portion of soup with a slice of lime or lemon. Makes 6 servings.

Sopa de Zanahoria
Carrot Soup

> 4 cups consommé
> 1 large onion, minced
> 2 tablespoons butter
> 3 tomatoes, peeled and diced
> 4 whole carrots, peeled
> Salt and pepper to taste

Bring the consommé to a boil. Meanwhile, sauté the onion in the butter until tender and transparent; add the tomatoes and simmer until thick. Then add the tomato mixture and the whole carrots to the boiling broth and simmer for about 30 minutes or until carrots are fork-tender. Remove carrots, crush them with a fork, and return to soup. Add salt and pepper to taste. Makes 6 servings.

Crema de Cebolla
Creamed Onion Soup

> 4 large yellow onions, thinly sliced
> 4 tablespoons butter
> 3 cups consommé
> 2 cups evaporated milk

2 cups water
Salt and pepper to taste

In a large soup kettle, gently sauté the onions in butter until limp and golden. Cover pan and cook over low heat for about 15 minutes. Add the consommé and the evaporated milk mixed with the water. Simmer for 5 or 10 minutes or until onions reach desired tenderness. Add salt and pepper to taste. Makes about 8 cups.

Sopa Mexicana
Mexican Soup

2 tablespoons butter
¼ cup chopped onions
1 large ripe tomato, peeled and chopped
1 teaspoon chopped parsley
1 cup cooked spinach, well chopped
2 quarts beef stock
Salt and pepper to taste
8 quartered tortillas, lightly fried
1 cup shredded romano cheese

In a soup kettle, heat the butter and sauté the onions until limp and golden. Add the tomato and parsley, and cook for a few minutes over low heat to blend flavors. Add spinach and the beef stock and bring to a boil. Add salt and pepper. Drop in the tortillas and ladle into soup bowls, sprinkling cheese over each portion. Makes 8 servings.

Sopa de Col Española
Spanish Cabbage Soup

4 strips bacon, diced
½ cup chopped onions

1 clove garlic, minced
2 cups sliced cabbage
½ cup tomato sauce
1½ quarts beef stock
1 bay leaf
2 potatoes, peeled and cubed
2 peppercorns
1 clove
Salt and pepper to taste
1 teaspoon vinegar

In a large soup pot, gently cook the diced bacon. When the fat is rendered, drain off all but 2 tablespoons and sauté the minced onions and garlic. When they turn limp and golden, add sliced cabbage and mix in. Then add tomato sauce. After 5 minutes add the stock and bay leaf and simmer for half an hour. Add the potatoes and continue cooking gently for about 15 minutes or until potatoes are done. Finally add the peppercorns, clove, salt, pepper, and vinegar. Serve very hot. Makes 8 servings.

Sopa de Ajo
Garlic Soup

3 tablespoons butter
12 cloves garlic, peeled
6 cups beef stock
3 sprigs parsley, minced
Salt and pepper to taste
3 egg yolks, well beaten
2 tablespoons olive oil
Croutons, toasted in butter
Grated Parmesan cheese

Melt the butter in a soup kettle and lightly sauté the garlic until soft. Add the stock, parsley, salt, and pepper. Boil slowly for about 30 minutes. Place the beaten egg yolks in a soup tureen and, drop by drop, beat in the olive oil (as in making mayonnaise). Then, a few drops at a time, beat a ladleful of the hot soup into the egg mixture. Pour in the rest of the soup through a strainer, pressing the juice out of the garlic. Fill soup bowls, adding croutons and a sprinkle of cheese to each serving. Makes 6 servings.

Sopa de Manzana
Apple Soup

> 2 tablespoons butter
> 1 small onion, chopped
> 1 tablespoon flour
> ½ cup tomato juice
> 1 quart chicken stock
> Salt and pepper to taste
> ⅓ cup dry sherry
> 2 medium apples, peeled and cut into small cubes
> Chopped parsley for garnish

In a soup kettle, heat the butter and sauté the onion until limp and golden. Mix in the flour and cook gently for a few minutes, stirring constantly. Add the tomato juice and simmer for a few minutes until flavors are blended. Add the chicken stock and the salt and pepper. Simmer for about 15 minutes. Remove from stove, add the wine and the cubed apples, and serve. Garnish each portion with chopped parsley. Makes 4 generous servings.

Sopa de Queso
Cheese Soup

> ¼ cup finely chopped raw carrots
> ½ cup finely chopped celery

½ stick butter
¼ cup chopped onions
¼ cup flour
2 cups milk
2 cups chicken stock
1 cup grated Cheddar cheese
Salt and pepper to taste
Chopped parsley for garnish

Place the carrots and celery in just enough lightly salted, boiling water to cover; cook until tender. Meanwhile, heat the butter in a large saucepan and gently sauté the onions until limp. Stir in the flour to make a paste and cook gently, without browning, for a few minutes. Carefully add the milk, a little at a time, stirring constantly, until the mixture thickens; then add the chicken stock, stirring constantly. When well blended, add the cooked, drained vegetables, then the cheese. Simmer gently, stirring slowly, until cheese is melted. Add salt and pepper to taste. Serve, garnished with chopped parsley. Makes 4 servings.

Sopa de Vino
Wine Soup

2 tablespoons butter
1 small onion, finely minced
2 tablespoons flour
1 medium tomato, peeled and chopped
5 cups chicken stock, heated
2 teaspoons salt
½ teaspoon pepper
2 tablespoons butter
2 slices dry white bread, cubed
3 hard-cooked eggs, quartered
1 cup red wine

Heat the butter, add onion, and sauté over medium heat until golden. Blend in flour until smooth, then stir in the tomato. Cover tightly and simmer for 10 minutes. Add tomato mixture to heated stock and simmer for 10 minutes. Add salt and pepper and taste to correct seasoning. Melt the butter, sauté the bread cubes, stirring for about 3 minutes or until evenly browned. Add the bread cubes, eggs, and wine to the soup and serve at once. Makes 8 servings.

Frijoles y Arroz
(Beans and Rice)

No Mexican meal is complete without beans in some form or another, for they're as much a part of the basic Mexican cuisine as chilies and tortillas.

Rice, too, is served in Mexico almost as often as beans and far oftener than pastas, although some typical Mexican recipes for these are also included here. No matter what the menu—enchiladas, tamales, meat, or chicken, it is nearly always flanked by beans and rice.

For that reason, I think both these important foods belong in the same chapter. So here we go—to tell you more about them and how to cook them in delicious ways as the Mexicans do.

BEANS

I've been told that there are close to a hundred varieties of beans throughout Mexico. While I can't vouch for the count, you can bet your sweet life that some kind of beans will show up at every Mexican meal. Usually they are served in a separate dish and on the soupy side unless they are refried beans.

To make a good pot of beans, you have to cook them right. First, they should be soaked for 8 hours and then simmered very, very slowly in a covered pot, preferably earthenware. If you use metal, make it stainless steel. Stir the beans occasionally while they're cooking and watch to be sure they haven't absorbed all the liquid, for beans will scorch very easily. If you need more liquid, bring it to a boil before adding it to the bean pot.

You can add onion and garlic right from the start, if you want, but don't add salt until the beans are done because salt toughens them. Mexican cooks usually add lard along with the salt after the beans are done and then continue cooking another half hour to blend in the flavors.

Cooking time can vary from 3½ to 6 hours, depending on altitude and hardness or softness of water, but 4 hours is about average. Beans begin to break open when they are done and you can test further by crushing a bean between your fingers. If it mashes easily, you're all set.

Here in the States, we have a good choice of beans, both packaged and canned, in our supermarkets and an even wider variety in Mexican, Puerto Rican, and Spanish grocery stores. And, by the way, beans are good for you. They're rich in B-complex vitamins, calcium, and protein, so it's great to be "full of beans."

Frijoles Refritos
Refried Beans

This dish is as characteristically Mexican as the tortilla. No matter where you go in Mexico or what the hour of the day, refried beans will turn up—at breakfast with your eggs, at luncheon or dinner, or tucked into a tortilla at the bullfights or at a street vendor's stand. These are beans that have been cooked, then mashed and fried, and in Mexico the frying is always done in lard. You can refrigerate any leftover refried beans and reheat them when wanted—thus the name, refried.

1 pound pinto or Mexican red beans
¼ pound salt pork, diced
2 cloves garlic, chopped
1 large onion, chopped
Boiling chicken stock to cover
Salt to taste
½ cup lard (or bacon fat) for frying
Grated Cheddar cheese

Soak beans in water for 8 hours or overnight; then drain off the water. In a large cooking pot, sauté the salt pork, add the garlic and onions; stir constantly until garlic is golden and the onions are transparent. Add drained beans to pork mixture and stir to coat the beans with the fat. Add enough boiling chicken stock to cover beans, stir once more, and bring to a boil. Cover, reduce the heat to very low, and simmer, stirring from time to time, to be sure beans won't stick to the bottom of the pot. If beans absorb all the liquid before they are done, add more chicken stock, but be sure to first heat it to boiling. Simmer for 4 hours, stirring occasionally. When done, season with salt to taste and let cook for 10 minutes more. Drain beans, saving the liquid.

In a large skillet or heavy kettle, heat the lard or bacon fat. Add some of the beans to the hot fat and mash thoroughly. Keep adding more beans and mashing, then add some of the liquid and more beans until all of the beans and liquid are used. Keep stirring and cooking until mashed bean mixture is thick and dry. To serve, top with grated Cheddar cheese. Makes 6 servings.

NOTE: You can add all kinds of flavors to this basic recipe for refried beans. If you like a touch of fire, add a teaspoon (or to taste) of crumbled and seeded dried pequín chili. Or add a cup of chopped canned tomatoes or 1 small can of tomato paste as part of the heated liquid.

Garbanzos con Jitomates
Chick-Peas with Tomatoes

You can use two 15-ounce cans drained garbanzo beans instead of cooking the dried garbanzos.

2 tablespoons butter
1 cup chopped onions
¼ cup chopped green pepper
4 cups cooked garbanzo beans
1 cup chicken stock
2 cups (No. 303 can) tomatoes, chopped
½ teaspoon salt
⅛ teaspoon pepper
¼ teaspoon orégano
1 bay leaf

Heat the butter in a large saucepan, and sauté the onions and green pepper until limp and tender. Stir in the garbanzos, chicken stock, tomatoes, salt, pepper, orégano, and bay leaf. Simmer, uncovered, for 30 minutes. Remove bay leaf before serving. Makes 6 servings.

Frijoles Borrachos
Drunken Beans

To precook the pinto beans, soak and simmer them as directed for the refried beans; then drain them, but do not mash.

½ cup chopped raw bacon
½ cup chopped onions
1 clove garlic, minced
¼ pound pork loin, cubed
2 cups (No. 303 can) tomatoes, chopped
1 pound Mexican pinto beans, precooked and drained
1 pint beer
Salt and pepper to taste

In a large skillet, gently fry the bacon until the fat is rendered. Add the onions and garlic and sauté in the bacon fat until limp and golden. Add the cubes of pork and turn them to brown on all sides. Add the tomatoes; cover tightly and simmer over low heat for about 30 minutes or until pork is tender. Stir in the beans and the beer; cover the skillet and simmer for another 15 or 20 minutes. Taste for seasoning and add salt and pepper. Makes 6 servings.

Frijoles Espesos
Creamy Beans

2 tablespoons lard or bacon fat
⅓ cup chopped onions
1 clove garlic, minced
2 tablespoons flour
1 cup chicken or beef stock
1 10½-ounce can red kidney beans, drained
1 4-inch link (¼ cup, if homemade) chorizo (sausage),
    skinned, fried, and crumbled
Salt and pepper to taste

In a skillet, heat the fat and sauté the onions and garlic until limp and golden. Mix in the flour and stir for about 3 minutes; then add the stock and stir until the sauce is smooth. Add the drained beans and simmer, stirring frequently, for about 15 or 20 minutes or until the beans start to fall apart and the mixture becomes custardy. Add more broth if necessary during the cooking. When done, add the fried, crumbled chorizo and let it heat through. Taste for seasoning and add salt and pepper if desired. Makes 4 servings.

RICE

For reasons that are not quite clear, the Mexicans call their rice and pasta dishes *sopas secas,* meaning dry soups. And these dry soups are traditionally served following the "wet" soup course at the main midday meal.

It surprises many people to find that Mexican cooks are as artful as the Chinese in preparing rice. However, as you might expect, the Mexicans season and embellish their rice and pasta dishes in all kinds of lively and delicious ways.

Arroz Mexicana—No. 1
Mexican Rice

½ stick butter
½ cup chopped onions
1 clove garlic, minced
2 tablespoons chopped green bell pepper
2 cups raw long grain white rice
1¾ cups (No. 300 can) tomato sauce
3 cups hot chicken stock
½ teaspoon monosodium glutamate
1 teaspoon salt
¼ teaspoon white pepper

In a large skillet or saucepan, heat half of the butter and gently sauté the onions, garlic, and green pepper until the onions are golden. Heat the rest of the butter in the same pan, add the rice, and cook gently, stirring constantly, until the rice is well coated and evenly colored. Add the tomato sauce and let heat through; then add the chicken stock. Cover and cook over low heat for 20 minutes or until the liquid has been absorbed. Season with monosodium glutamate, salt, and pepper. Makes 6 servings.

Arroz Mexicana—No. 2

Here's another version of this popular dish.

2 4-inch links chorizo sausage, sliced
3 tablespoons butter
2 cups raw long grain white rice
⅓ cup tomato purée
1 teaspoon onion juice
½ cup cooked green peas
3 cups beef stock
1 teaspoon salt or to taste
Chopped parsley
2 hard-cooked eggs, sliced
2 avocados, peeled and sliced

Slick a skillet with just enough oil to keep the sausage from sticking; then fry the chorizo slices for about 10 minutes or until well done; remove from pan and keep warm. Drain all but 1 tablespoon of fat from pan. Add the butter, heat and sauté the rice until well coated and golden. Add the tomato purée and onion juice and let simmer until rice is dry. Stir in the peas, add the beef stock and salt; cover and let simmer for about 20 minutes, or until all the liquid has been absorbed and rice is tender. Turn onto a serving plate and garnish with parsley and slices of fried chorizos, hard-cooked eggs, and avocado. Makes 6 servings.

Arroz Verde
Green Rice

>3 sweet bell peppers, seeded and cut up
>2 large sprigs of parsley
>1 large onion, chopped
>1 clove garlic, chopped
>4 cups chicken stock
>¾ stick butter
>2 cups raw long grain white rice
>Salt and pepper to taste

Place the green peppers in the electric blender along with the parsley, onion, garlic, and ¼ cup of the stock. Blend until smoothly puréed. Heat the butter in a large saucepan and gently sauté the rice until it is well coated and golden. Add the purée and gently cook for another 5 minutes. Add the rest of the stock; cover; bring to a boil and quickly reduce heat. Let simmer until all the liquid has been absorbed and rice is tender. Add salt and pepper to taste. Makes 6 servings.

Tallarines con Perejil y Queso
Parsley Cheese Noodles

>1 8-ounce package medium-thin noodles
>1 cup cream-style cottage cheese
>¼ cup chopped parsley
>⅛ teaspoon garlic powder
>¼ cup melted butter
>¼ cup crumbled blue cheese
>¼ cup grated onion
>¼ teaspoon white pepper
>1 teaspoon salt
>3 eggs, well beaten
>Paprika

Cook noodles according to package directions and drain.

Combine noodles with cottage cheese and rest of ingredients except eggs and paprika. Toss lightly and stir in beaten eggs. Pour into a well-greased casserole and bake in a preheated oven at 350° F. for 30 minutes. Sprinkle lightly with paprika before serving. Makes about 6 servings.

Tallarines con Salsa Picante
Noodles with Hot Sauce

> 1 8-ounce package noodles
> 2 tablespoons butter
> Salt to taste
> 2 cups tomato sauce
> 2 teaspoons minced parsley
> 1 tablespoon minced onion
> 2 teaspoons chili powder or to taste
> 4 cooked link pork sausages, sliced
> ¾ cup grated Parmesan cheese
> Butter

Boil noodles according to package directions and drain well. Stir in the 2 tablespoons butter and salt to taste. In a saucepan, mix the tomato sauce with the parsley, onion, and chili powder and simmer for 5 minutes; add sliced sausage. In a well-buttered casserole, alternate layers of noodles, sauce with sausage, and grated cheese, finishing with a layer of noodles. Dot with butter and sprinkle with cheese. Bake, uncovered, in a preheated 350° F. oven for about 15 minutes or until top is browned. Makes about 6 servings.

Macarrón con Chorizos
Macaroni with Sausage

> 1 8-ounce package macaroni
> 1 small onion, stuck with 2 cloves

3 peppercorns
½ bay leaf
2 4-inch links (½ cup if homemade) chorizo (sausage),
    skinned and sliced, or 4 pork sausage links,
    sliced
1 small pat butter
1 medium onion, finely chopped
1 cup (8-ounce can) tomatoes, diced
1 tablespoon chopped parsley
Salt and pepper to taste
½ cup grated Parmesan cheese

Cook macaroni according to package directions, adding to the water the small onion, peppercorns and bay leaf. When done, rinse in cold water and drain; remove bay leaf and onion. Fry the sausage slices in the butter for about 10 minutes or until brown; remove from pan and set aside. Drain off all but 2 tablespoons of fat and sauté the chopped onion till golden; add the tomatoes, parsley, salt, and pepper, and simmer until thickened. In a well-buttered baking dish, alternate layers of macaroni, sliced sausage, the tomato sauce and grated cheese, ending with a topping of cheese. Bake in a preheated 350° F. oven for about 20 minutes. Makes about 6 servings.

Sopa Seca de Fideos con Setas
Vermicelli and Mushroom Casserole

¾ stick butter
1 8-ounce package vermicelli
1 small onion, minced
1 clove garlic, minced
2 cups sliced fresh mushrooms
1 8-ounce can tomatoes, diced
2 cups chicken stock
Salt and pepper to taste

1 tablespoon chopped parsley
1 cup freshly grated Parmesan or romano cheese

Heat half of the butter in a skillet and sauté the vermicelli, stirring constantly, until well coated and golden; then place in a casserole. In the same skillet, heat the rest of the butter and sauté onion, garlic, and mushrooms until limp and tender. Add tomatoes, chicken stock, salt, pepper, and parsley and bring mixture just to a boil; then pour over the vermicelli. Cover with grated cheese and bake, uncovered, in preheated 325° F. oven for about 15 minutes. Makes about 6 servings.

Sopa Seca de Tortilla con Queso
Tortilla and Cheese Casserole

1 medium onion, chopped
1 clove garlic, chopped
1 stick butter
1 1-pound can tomatoes, drained and mashed
½ teaspoon orégano
Salt and pepper to taste
12 tortillas, cut in narrow strips
1 cup heavy cream
1 cup (about ¼ pound) freshly grated Parmesan cheese

Sauté the onion and garlic in half of the butter until tender and golden. Add the tomatoes and seasoning, and cook, stirring, until the sauce is smooth and the flavors blended. Remove from heat and set aside.

Heat the remaining butter in a skillet and gently fry the tortilla strips without letting them get brown or crisp. Drain on paper towels. In a well-buttered casserole, alternate layers of sauce, tortilla strips, cream, and grated cheese, ending with the cheese. Bake in preheated 350° F. oven for about 15 minutes or until heated through. Makes 6 servings.

Huevos
[Eggs]

When it comes to creative cooking, you just can't beat the opportunities offered by eggs. They blend with every flavor you can think of, and almost every kind of food goes well with eggs.

One of my favorite dishes in this chapter is Huevos Texas-Mex, scrambled eggs with smoked salmon. And there are some terrific omelet recipes, too. You can't beat these recipes for a quick luncheon dish when unexpected guests come by. With eggs on hand plus a few cans of tomato sauce and chilies, there's no reason to go into a tiz about what to serve. Look through this chapter and see how many good egg dishes you can whip up in no time.

Señor Pico Huevos Rancheros
Mexican Ranch Style Eggs

There are as many variations of Huevos Rancheros as there are Mexican cooks, but give or take a change or two, it's one helluva dish. Serve it with refried beans and rice—as they do South of the Border—or, if you prefer, with crisp bacon or sausage.

> 4 tortillas
> Butter for frying
> 8 eggs
> 2 cups Ranchero Sauce (recipe follows)
> ½ cup grated Monterey Jack cheese
> Avocado slices

Soft-toast the tortillas and keep warm. Heat the butter in a skillet and gently fry the eggs until the whites are set. Pour 1 cup of the Ranchero Sauce over eggs and cook over low heat for several minutes. Place one tortilla on each plate; lift 2 eggs onto each tortilla. Distribute the remaining cup of sauce over the top of each portion and top with a sprinkling of cheese. Garnish the plates with avocado slices. Makes 4 servings.

NOTE: Instead of frying the eggs, they may be poached in the sauce and served in the same manner.

RANCHERO SAUCE

> 1 small onion, finely chopped
> 1 clove garlic, minced
> 1 tablespoon oil or butter
> 1 canned small green chili, chopped
> 1 cup chicken stock
> 1 cup tomato sauce
> ½ teaspoon orégano
> Salt and pepper to taste

To make the sauce, sauté the onion and garlic in the oil or butter until limp. Add the chili, chicken stock, tomato sauce, and orégano; simmer for 5 minutes or so until flavors are well blended. Season with salt and pepper. Keep warm until needed. Makes 2 cups sauce.

Señor Pico Omelet

>2 4-inch links (or ½ cup, if homemade) chorizo sausage
>1 cup crushed tostadas
>½ cup nopalitos (cactus pieces), rinsed and drained
>2 tablespoons butter
>8 eggs, well beaten
>2 cups Señor Pico Sauce for Chiles Rellenos, heated (see Index)

Skin the chorizo links and fry them in an oil-slicked skillet for about 10 minutes, crumbling with a fork, until well browned. Drain off the fat; then mix the sausage with the tostadas and the nopalitos. In another skillet, heat the butter, add the eggs and cook gently, lifting the edges occasionally to let the uncooked part run underneath. When omelet is set, spread on the sausage mixture, fold over, and place on heated serving platter. Pour on the heated sauce. Makes 4 to 6 servings.

Tortilla de Huevos con Alcachofas
Artichoke Omelet

>6 canned artichoke hearts, rinsed and drained
>2 medium onions, sliced in fine rings
>2 tablespoons butter
>8 eggs, slightly beaten
>3 tablespoons milk
>½ cup soft bread crumbs

3 tablespoons grated Parmesan cheese
2 tablespoons chopped parsley
Salt and pepper to taste

Slice the artichoke hearts and gently sauté them with the onions in melted butter until they are just heated through. Blend the beaten eggs with the milk, bread crumbs, cheese, parsley, salt, and pepper. Pour the egg mixture over the artichoke hearts and onions. Cook gently, lifting the edges occasionally to let the uncooked part run underneath. When omelet is set, fold over and place on hot platter to serve. Makes 4 to 6 servings.

Tortilla de Huevos con Aguacates
Avocado Omelet

1½ cups sour cream
1 teaspoon salt
¼ teaspoon pepper
2 large tomatoes, peeled and chopped
1 avocado, peeled and diced
8 eggs, slightly beaten
⅓ cup milk
½ teaspoon salt
2 tablespoons butter

Heat sour cream, salt, and pepper in double boiler. Add tomatoes and avocado. Heat for another 5 minutes. Meanwhile, blend the beaten eggs with the milk and salt. Pour into heated butter in skillet and cook gently, lifting edges occasionally to let uncooked part run underneath. When set, pour half of sauce mixture over omelet and fold over. Place on hot platter and pour on the rest of the sauce. Makes 4 to 6 servings.

Tortilla de Huevos Española
Spanish Omelet

        4 slices bacon
        ½ green bell pepper, seeded and chopped
        1 medium onion, finely chopped
        ½ clove garlic, minced
        4 large mushrooms, chopped
        1 tomato, peeled and finely chopped
        8 eggs
        ½ teaspoon each salt and pepper
        ⅓ cup light cream
        2 tablespoons butter
        2 cups canned Spanish-style tomato sauce, heated

Cut bacon into small pieces and fry gently until crisp; remove from pan and keep warm. Leave 2 tablespoons bacon fat in skillet and sauté the green pepper, onion, garlic, and mushrooms until soft and tender. Add the tomato and cook gently for about 10 minutes until flavors are well blended. Beat the eggs with the salt, pepper, and cream until fluffy. Let the butter heat to sizzling in a skillet, reduce heat, and cook the omelet slowly. As it begins to set, lift the edges with a spatula to let the uncooked portion flow underneath and cook. When set, sprinkle the bacon pieces and the tomato mixture over half of the omelet and fold over. Place on a heated serving dish and pass the heated tomato sauce on the side. Makes 4 to 6 servings.

Señor Pico Huevos Maximiliano
Señor Pico Eggs Maximilian

        ½ cup finely chopped onions
        ½ cup finely chopped green pepper
        ½ stick butter
        2 tomatoes, peeled and diced

2 tablespoons nopalitos (cactus pieces)
2 tablespoons chopped, canned jalapeño chili, seeded,
  rinsed, and drained
Salt and pepper to taste
8 thin slices ham or Canadian bacon
8 Holland Rusks, buttered
8 eggs, beaten
2 tablespoons butter
1 teaspoon salt
½ teaspoon pepper
8 pitted black olives, cut in half

Sauté onions and green pepper in the butter. When limp and tender, add tomatoes, nopalitos, chili, salt, and pepper. Cook slowly over low heat for about 5 minutes or until well blended, and keep warm until needed. Sauté or grill the ham or Canadian bacon slices and place on buttered Holland Rusks. Scramble the eggs in the butter, adding salt and pepper, and distribute them on top of the Holland Rusks, allowing 2 per serving. Distribute the vegetable mixture on top of the eggs and garnish with olive halves. Makes 4 luncheon-size servings.

Huevos con Calabacitas
Scrambled Eggs with Zucchini

3 tablespoons butter
2 cups coarsely chopped raw zucchini
½ teaspoon chili powder
Salt and pepper to taste
6 eggs
2 tablespoons light cream
1 cup grated Monterey Jack cheese
1½ tablespoons butter
Chopped chives

In a saucepan, melt the butter, add the zucchini, and cook, covered, for about 10 minutes, stirring occasionally, until the zucchini is tender but not mushy. Drain the zucchini; season with chili powder, salt, and pepper, and keep it warm. Beat the eggs with the cream, stir in the grated cheese, and scramble them in the butter over low heat. Before eggs begin to set, stir in the zucchini and continue to scramble until eggs are done. Makes 4 servings.

Huevos con Nopalitos
Scrambled Eggs with Cactus

> 1 8-ounce can nopalitos (cactus pieces)
> 3 tablespoons butter
> 2 tablespoons light cream
> Salt and pepper to taste
> 8 eggs, lightly beaten

Rinse nopalitos thoroughly and drain well. When dry, sauté them gently in the butter. Blend the cream and the salt and pepper into the beaten eggs and scramble them into the nopalitos. Makes 4 servings.

Huevos con Tortillas
Scrambled Eggs with Tortillas

> 3 tablespoons butter
> ¼ cup finely chopped onions
> 8 tortillas, cut into the size of potato chips
> 2 medium tomatoes, peeled and cubed
> 8 eggs, well beaten
> Salt and pepper to taste
> ¼ cup grated Parmesan cheese
> 2 tablespoons chopped parsley

Heat the butter in a skillet and sauté the onions until tender and golden. Add the tortilla pieces and gently brown them just a little bit. Then stir in the tomatoes and let the mixture heat through. Add the beaten eggs and scramble them in to the tomato mixture, adding salt and pepper to taste. Serve at once, topping each portion with the grated cheese and a sprinkle of parsley. Makes 4 to 6 servings.

Huevos Texas-Mex
Scrambled Eggs Texas-Mex Style

This recipe was given to me by my good friend Hayden Head, of Corpus Christi, Texas, who cooks up some mighty good inventions when the spirit moves him. If you like smoked salmon as much as I do, you'll want to add this dish to your list of favorites for brunch. If smoked salmon is a little too rich for your wallet, you can substitute the same amount of well-drained canned salmon, but I'll have to warn you—it won't have quite the same oomph.

½ stick butter
1 large onion, finely chopped
3 medium tomatoes, peeled and chopped
1 tablespoon Texas sweet-hot relish
1 dozen eggs, lightly beaten
1½ cups diced or julienned smoked salmon

Heat the butter in a large skillet and sauté the onion until limp and transparent. Stir in the tomatoes and the relish and cook for a few minutes to let flavors blend. Scramble in the eggs and add the salmon at the very last to just let it heat through. The mixture should be well enough seasoned, but you can taste to see if you want to add salt and pepper. Makes 6 to 8 servings.

Huevos con Cecina
Scrambled Eggs with Dried Beef

> 3 tablespoons butter
> 1 2½-ounce jar dried beef
> 1 cup canned tomatoes, cut up
> 1 teaspoon chili powder
> 1 3-ounce package cream cheese, diced
> 8 eggs, beaten
> Salt and pepper to taste

Heat the butter in a skillet and quickly brown the beef slices without letting them get hard or crisp. Remove the beef and keep it warm. In the same skillet, place the tomatoes, add the chili powder, and when heated through add the cream cheese. Cook slowly over medium heat, stirring, until the mixture is smooth and starts to bubble. Stir in the beef slices, then the beaten eggs, and scramble. Add salt and pepper to taste if desired. Makes 4 to 6 servings.

Huevos con Frijoles
Poached Eggs with Beans

> ½ pound dried pinto beans
> 2 small onions, finely chopped
> 1 clove garlic, minced
> ½ stick butter
> 1 cup canned Spanish-style tomato sauce
> 4 eggs, poached
> ¼ cup shredded Parmesan cheese
> 2 tablespoons melted butter

Soak the beans overnight and cook as directed on the package. Sauté the onions and garlic in the butter until limp and golden. Add the cooked beans and tomato sauce and simmer gently for about 10 minutes for flavors to blend. Transfer the mixture to a baking dish, top with the poached eggs, sprinkle on the grated cheese and melted butter. Place in a preheated 400° F. oven for 2 or 3 minutes and serve while bubbling hot. Makes 4 servings.

Huevos al Horno con Queso
Baked Eggs with Cheese Sauce

This is a fast way to whip up a brunch dish. It tastes great and can be adjusted to serve any number of people.

> 6 teaspoons butter
> 6 teaspoons light cream
> 6 eggs
> Salt and pepper to taste
> 6 tortillas
> 1 can Campbell's Cheddar cheese soup
> ½ to 1 canned Ortega chili, chopped

Into a muffin pan (preferably Teflon-coated for ease of removing eggs) or into custard cups, put 1 teaspoon each of butter and cream. Place in a preheated 325° F. oven for 5 to 10 minutes or until pan is heated and butter melted. Break an egg into each pan or cup; sprinkle with salt and pepper and bake for about 10 minutes or until whites are set; remove from oven and let stand a minute or two. While eggs are baking, soft-toast the tortillas and keep warm. Heat the soup and stir in the chopped chili. Assemble each serving by placing one egg (remove from baking dish with a spatula) on each tortilla and spooning on the cheese sauce. Makes 6 servings.

Huevos con Arroz al Horno
Baked Eggs with Rice

> ½ stick butter
> 1 large onion, finely chopped

½ cup raw white rice
2 cups beef stock
1 teaspoon salt
1 teaspoon chili powder
6 strips bacon, partially fried but not crisp
6 eggs
Grated Parmesan cheese

In a skillet, heat the butter and sauté the onion until limp; then push onion to one side. Add the rice and sauté until well coated and golden. Add the stock and the seasonings and stir until well blended. Turn mixture into a buttered casserole; cover and bake in a preheated 350° F. oven for about 30 minutes or until liquid is absorbed. Uncover; form 6 nests of rice, wrapping each with bacon strip (fasten bacon with toothpick); break 1 egg into each hollow. Sprinkle each egg generously with Parmesan cheese; replace casserole in oven for about 8 to 10 minutes or until eggs are set but still tender. Makes 6 servings.

Huevos con Frijoles al Horno
Mexican Eggs

A good luncheon dish, served with a green salad and ice-cold beer.

½ cup prepared refried beans
4 eggs
4 tortillas
2 tablespoons minced onions
1 cup grated Cheddar cheese
Salsa Borracha (see Index)

Preheat oven to 375° F. Place the refried beans in covered ovenware and let them heat in 375° F. oven. While beans heat, fry or poach the eggs just until the whites are set. Place the tortillas on a cookie sheet and on each one spread 2 tablespoons heated beans; then top with a partially cooked egg. Sprinkle each egg with ½ tablespoon onion and ¼ cup grated cheese. Return to the oven for 4 to 5 minutes, or until cheese melts and is bubbly. Pass the Salsa Borracha in a serving dish. Makes 4 servings.

Soufflé de Queso con Chorizo
Cheese and Chorizo Soufflé

2 4-inch links (½ cup if homemade) chorizo sausage
½ cup masa harina (corn meal)
2 cups milk
1 tablespoon butter
4 large eggs, separated
1 cup grated Cheddar cheese
¼ teaspoon salt

Skin the chorizo links and crumble them into a heated skillet slicked with oil to keep the sausage from sticking. Stir-fry until firm; drain chorizo thoroughly on paper towels. In a saucepan, mix corn meal with milk; add butter and heat just to boiling. Reduce heat and simmer, stirring frequently, for 5 minutes or until quite thick. Beat egg yolks, stir in a little of the hot corn meal, and return egg yolks to saucepan, stirring for about a minute to allow eggs to thicken. Remove from heat; add grated cheese and stir to melt. Add well-crumbled chorizo and let mixture cool to lukewarm. Add salt to egg whites and beat until stiff but not dry. Fold egg whites into corn meal mixture very gently; pour into ungreased casserole. Bake in preheated 350° F. oven for about 50 minutes or until crusty on top and firm in the center. Makes about 4 servings.

Huevos con Salsa de Aguacates
Hard-Cooked Eggs with Avocado Sauce

8 hot hard-cooked eggs
¼ cup heavy cream
1 tablespoon cornstarch
½ teaspoon chili powder
Salt and pepper to taste
3 very ripe avocados, peeled, mashed, and sieved
4 slices buttered toast
Paprika
Chopped chives

While the eggs are cooking, make the sauce. Warm the cream over low heat. Stir in the cornstarch and add the chili powder, salt, and pepper. Simmer over low heat (do not allow to boil), stirring constantly, for about 5 minutes or until sauce is thickened. Add the sieved avocados and simmer gently for another 5 or so minutes, stirring constantly, until sauce is thick and creamy. Quarter the eggs (allowing two hard-cooked eggs per serving) and distribute them on the slices of hot buttered toast. Top each serving with the avocado sauce and sprinkle on a garnish of paprika and chopped chives. Makes 4 servings.

Pescado
(Fish)

Fish is my idea of soul food. I love it and I often eat it twice a day. So I'm in seventh heaven when I travel in Mexico, where the country's two long coastlines and many inland lakes offer an endless variety of marvelous shellfish as well as ocean and fresh water fish.

I remember a day in Baja California, when my bride and I caught seventeen different kinds of fish, among them two tuna about fifteen pounds apiece. Some young friends of ours, visiting from Hawaii, asked me to make them some *sashimi* from the tuna, which consists of raw slices of fish with soya sauce and hot, hot mustard or *wasabi* powder. This is the Japanese version of Mexican *ceviche*, for which I've given you a recipe, where the raw fish is "cooked" in lime juice and seasonings. That day we really feasted on a meal fresh from the ocean. On the other hand, you can also feast on my recipe for Señor Pico Spaghetti Las Cruces, which comes right from the cans on your pantry shelf. What I want to get across is that whether your fish comes directly from lakes, streams, or oceans—or whether it comes from your neighborhood grocery store—it can be a memorable meal.

You'll notice in this chapter that Mexican cooks use red snapper for a good many of these recipes. In most cases, any firm, white-fleshed fish can be substituted. In our Señor Pico restaurants, we often use mahimahi, but since you can't always get this at your fish market, fresh halibut or cod will make a better substitute than fillet of sole.

Just remember one thing: while different kinds of fish take different lengths of time in the cooking, too many people overcook it. So watch the clock or you'll end up with a texture like the eraser on your pencil.

Señor Pico Ceviche
Marinated Raw Fish

The Hawaiians have their *lomi lomi*, the Tahitians their *poisson cru*, and the Mexicans have their *ceviche*, which is also fish "cooked" in fresh lime juice. The seasonings may vary but the principle is the same, and all are delicious to the initiated. In this country we eat raw oysters and cherrystone or littleneck clams on the half shell. The Japanese eat sashimi. So eating raw fish marinated in lime juice isn't as outlandish as it sounds.

The Mexicans use Spanish mackerel or *corbina* for their ceviche, but you can choose any of the white-flesh fish that are less fat. The following recipe is basic, but it can be varied with your own seasonings once you have made it and know what to expect. Green pepper may be added or wine vinegar and a little olive oil. A pinch of orégano would do the dish no harm.

1 pound raw mahimahi, or any fine-textured white fish,
 diced
1 teaspoon sugar
2 teaspoons salt
1 teaspoon monosodium glutamate
1 pinch orégano
1 teaspoon white pepper
4 dashes Tabasco sauce
2 tablespoons finely chopped onions
Juice of four large limes
2 cups peeled and diced tomatoes

Marinate diced raw fish with seasonings and onions in lime juice for 3 to 4 hours. Add tomatoes and chill thoroughly. Serve with cocktails or as an opening course using small dishes with cocktail forks. Makes 8 servings for a first course.

Pescado Frío con Guacamole
Cold Fish with Avocado Sauce

6 to 8 slices fresh fish fillets of any firm white fish
Salt and pepper to taste
3 teaspoons dried tarragon, crumbled
¼ cup fresh lime juice
2 tablespoons butter
2 fresh tomatoes, peeled and chopped
3 very ripe avocados, mashed
2 tablespoons minced onions
2 teaspoons chili powder or to taste
2½ tablespoons minced parsley
1 clove garlic, crushed
1 tablespoon olive oil
13 black olives, pitted and sliced
1 can sweet red peppers, cut into strips

Sprinkle the fish fillets with salt, pepper, and tarragon and soak in lime juice for a few minutes. Arrange fish in a buttered baking dish and bake in a preheated 350° F. oven for about 25 minutes or until it flakes easily with a fork. While fish is baking, combine the remaining ingredients except the last two. Let the fish cool. When ready to serve, spread the cool fillets with the avocado sauce and garnish with the sliced olives and strips of sweet red pepper. Makes 6 to 8 servings.

Pescado en Escabeche al Horno
Baked Fish Vinaigrette

In downtown Guadalajara, one floor up and overlooking the street, is a charming little restaurant called Copa de Leche, which means "cup of milk." It was there that I had the most fabulous mixture of fish, seasonings, and vegetables. Called *escabeche,* it is sort of a Mexican antipasto.

2 pounds small whole smelts, sardines, mullets, or any
   small whole fish
Flour
Oil for deep frying
½ cup olive oil
2 cloves garlic, minced
2 large onions, sliced very thin
¼ cup canned jalapeño chilies, seeded, rinsed, drained,
   and chopped
2 green bell peppers, seeded and chopped
¼ teaspoon cuminseed
½ teaspoon orégano
½ teaspoon peppercorns, crushed
2 teaspoons salt
2 bay leaves
1½ cups white wine vinegar
Pimiento strips
Ripe olives

Wash and clean the fish; leave heads and tails intact; roll in flour and deep-fry in hot oil for 5 to 10 seconds until lightly browned. Remove and arrange in earthenware or Pyrex casserole. In a skillet, heat the ½ cup olive oil and sauté garlic and onions until soft. Add chilies, green peppers, seasonings and wine vinegar. Bring to a boil, then reduce heat and simmer for 10 minutes. Pour over fish. Let cool; then cover and refrigerate 24 hours. To serve, garnish with pimiento and ripe olives. Makes 4 to 6 servings.

The same sauce may be used for poached or baked fish fillets or steaks.

Pescado al Horno Yucatán
Baked Fish Yucatán Style

3 tablespoons butter
1 medium onion, chopped
½ sweet red pepper, seeded and chopped
⅔ cup sliced pimiento-stuffed olives
2 tablespoons chopped parsley
Juice of 2 oranges
½ teaspoon salt
Freshly ground black pepper to taste
1 5-pound whole red snapper, cleaned, with head and
    tail left on
2 hard-cooked eggs, finely chopped

Heat butter in a skillet and sauté the onion until limp and golden. Stir in the chopped pepper, olives, and parsley and cook for another few minutes. Add the orange juice, salt, and pepper and let simmer a minute or two for flavors to blend; remove from heat.

Place the fish in a well-buttered baking pan, pour the sauce over it, and bake, uncovered, for about 30 minutes in a preheated 400° F. oven, basting occasionally with the pan sauce. When done, transfer the fish to a heated serving platter, pour the sauce over it, and garnish with the chopped eggs. Makes 8 servings.

Huachinago Veracruzano
Red Snapper Veracruz Style

While this dish is said to have originated in Veracruz, it is a favorite throughout Mexico and is usually served with boiled potatoes. The red snapper, so popular with Mexicans, is the traditional fish for this recipe, but any firm white fish may be used.

6 red snapper fillets (about 2½ to 3 pounds)
Salt and pepper
4 tablespoons fresh lime or lemon juice

SAUCE

3 cups canned tomatoes or fresh tomatoes, peeled and
    diced
2 tablespoons cooking oil
¾ cup coarsely chopped onions
2 cloves garlic, minced
3 to 4 pickled (en escabeche) jalapeño chilies, seeded,
    rinsed, and cut into strips
¼ cup pimiento-stuffed olives, sliced
1 teaspoon salt
1 pinch cinnamon
1 pinch clove

Sprinkle the fish fillets with salt and pepper, brush with lime or lemon juice, and let stand while you prepare the sauce. Mash the tomatoes or purée them in the blender. Heat the oil in a skillet and sauté the onions and garlic until tender and golden. Add the tomatoes and the remaining ingredients and cook gently over moderate heat for about 5 minutes. Place the fish fillets in a greased casserole. Pour on the sauce, cover, and bake in a preheated 350° F. oven for about 20 to 30 minutes, or until fish flakes easily with a fork.

To serve, transfer the fish to a heated platter, surrounded, if you like, with boiled potatoes, and pour sauce over all. Makes 6 servings.

Señor Pico Halibut Veracruz

    6 fresh halibut fillets
    1 cup dry white wine
    1 cup fish stock, or
        ½ cup clam juice mixed with ½ cup water
    3 tablespoons butter
    2 tablespoons finely chopped onions
    1 green bell pepper, seeded and julienned
    3 canned green chilies, rinsed, seeded, and julienned
    3 medium-sized tomatoes, peeled and diced
    2 tablespoons julienned pimiento
    1 cup (1 8-ounce can) white sauce
    12 pitted green olives, sliced
    12 pitted black olives, sliced
    Salt and white pepper to taste

Poach the halibut in a mixture of the wine and fish stock or clam juice for about 12 minutes or until fish flakes easily with a fork. Transfer the fillets to a serving platter and keep warm; reserve the stock. Heat the butter in a skillet and sauté the onions, green pepper, and chilies until the onions are limp and transparent. Add tomatoes and pimiento; let simmer until hot. Add all of the stock in which the fish was poached and the white sauce. Let simmer and stir until flavors are well blended; stir in olives and season to taste. Pour over fish fillets and serve. Makes 6 servings.

Pescado en Vino Blanco
Fish in White Wine

> 1 whole sea bass, about 4 pounds
> Flour seasoned with salt and pepper
> ½ stick butter
> 1 large onion, finely chopped
> 2 cups dry white wine
> ⅛ teaspoon allspice
> Salt and pepper to taste
> 2 tablespoons chopped parsley
> Lemon juice

Dust the fish in the seasoned flour. In a large skillet, heat the butter and sauté the fish on both sides until lightly browned; then transfer it to a buttered flameproof casserole with a cover.

Sauté the onion in the butter remaining in the skillet until tender and golden; add to the casserole. Mix the wine, allspice, salt, pepper, and parsley and pour over the fish. Cover, and simmer very gently over a very low heat for about 25 minutes or until the fish flakes easily when tested with a fork. When ready to serve, sprinkle the fish generously with lemon juice. Makes about 6 servings.

Pescado en Vino Tinto
Fish in Red Wine Sauce

Make the sauce for this dish as far ahead as several days, if possible, for the longer it stands, the better the good flavors will marry.

> 2 pounds sea bass or any ocean fish, sliced

SAUCE

1 cup dry red wine
½ cup olive oil
1 cup (1 can) tomato sauce
1 clove garlic, minced
1 teaspoon salt
¼ teaspoon pepper
1 teaspoon orégano
1 sweet red pepper, seeded and cut into thin strips
3 tablespoons chopped parsley
1 cup sliced green olives
1 tablespoon capers

Mix all the ingredients for the sauce and let stand at least 1 hour, but longer if time permits. Taste and correct seasoning.

When ready to cook, place the fish slices, without overlapping, in a casserole that has a cover. Pour on the sauce, cover the casserole, and bake in a preheated 350° F. oven for about 20 to 30 minutes or until fish flakes easily with a fork. Makes 4 servings.

Pescado en Salsa de Almendra
Fish in Almond Sauce

6 fillets of any firm white fish
2 tablespoons lemon juice
Salt and pepper to taste
¼ cup melted butter
1 cup ground blanched almonds
½ cup milk
½ cup light sherry
1 cup grated Monterey Jack cheese

¼ cup bread crumbs
Pinch of allspice
Salt and pepper
Butter

Brush the fish fillets with the lemon juice, sprinkle lightly with salt and pepper and let stand for 30 minutes. Then place the fillets side by side in a buttered baking dish and brush them with the melted butter. Blend together the ground almonds, milk, sherry, and grated cheese, and pour the mixture over the fish slices. Sprinkle with the bread crumbs, allspice, salt, and pepper; dot with butter. Bake, uncovered, in a preheated 400° F. oven for about 30 minutes or until fish flakes easily with a fork. Makes 6 servings.

Pescado en Salsa de Nuez
Fish in Walnut Sauce

6 fillets of halibut or sole
1 cup dry white wine
1 10-ounce can Mexican green tomatoes
2 small onions, chopped
1 clove garlic, mashed
Salt and pepper to taste
1 cup walnuts
2 canned serrano chilies*
2 sprigs parsley, chopped
Juice of half a lemon

Rinse the fish fillets, pat dry on paper towels, and set aside. In a saucepan, mix the wine, 1 cup of the liquid from the canned green tomatoes, the onions, garlic, salt, and pepper. Simmer for about 30 minutes to make a court bouillon. Strain the bouillon into a poaching pan, reserving the onion and garlic for later use. Bring the bouillon to a rapid boil, add the fish fillets, and immediately reduce the heat. Poach the fillets at a simmer for about 6 to 12 minutes (depending on thickness of fillets or until the fish flakes easily with a fork). Transfer the fillets to a heated serving platter and keep warm.

Place all the court bouillon, including the reserved onion and garlic, in a blender with the remaining ingredients, blending a portion at a time if container space is limited, and blend until smooth. Heat the sauce but do not let it boil. When hot, pour over the fish fillets and serve at once. Makes 6 servings.

* The small serrano chilies are quite fiery, and you may prefer to use 1 canned green chili, which is much larger but milder. The green chili should also be seeded, rinsed, and chopped before blending.

Pescado a la Española
Fish Spanish Style

  6 fillets of sole
  1 teaspoon salt
  ½ bay leaf
  1 slice lemon
  3 tablespoons olive oil
  2 tablespoons minced onion
  1 clove garlic
  4 tomatoes, peeled and chopped
  Salt and pepper to taste
  ¼ cup halved blanched almonds
  ½ cup raisins, soaked in white wine to cover
  1 tablespoon capers
  1 tablespoon vinegar

Simmer the fillets for about 6 minutes in just enough water to cover along with the salt, bay leaf, and lemon slice. Remove fillets from the stock and set all aside. In a large skillet, heat the oil and sauté the onion and garlic until limp and golden. Stir in the chopped tomatoes and cook gently for a few minutes. Add ¾ cup of the fish stock, salt and pepper to taste, and cook over moderate heat for a few minutes until flavors are blended. Add

TRADER VIC'S BOOK OF MEXICAN COOKING

the fillets and the rest of the ingredients, cooking just long enough to heat through. Makes 6 servings.

Pescado con Salsa de Perejil
Fish with Parsley Sauce

>   4 fillets of halibut or other white fish
>   Juice of 1 lemon
>   Salt and pepper
>   1 teaspoon dried tarragon
>   ½ stick butter
>   1 small onion, finely chopped
>   1 clove garlic, minced
>   1 large bunch parsley, coarsely chopped
>   1½ cups dry white wine
>   Salt and pepper to taste

Rub the fillets on each side with lemon juice; sprinkle lightly with salt, pepper, and tarragon; let stand for about 30 minutes. Meanwhile, heat the butter in a skillet and sauté the onion, garlic, and parsley until the onion is limp and golden. Add the wine and simmer for a few minutes until flavors are blended; then add salt and pepper to taste. Place fillets in a buttered baking dish, pour the wine sauce over them, and bake in a preheated 350° F. oven for about 30 minutes or until the fish flakes easily with a fork. Baste the fillets with their pan sauce several times during the baking, adding a little more wine if necessary. Makes 4 servings.

Salsa de Pasas Para Pescado
Raisin Sauce for Fish

Here is an unusual and mighty tasty sauce that goes well with any of the white-fleshed fish. Poach or bake your fillets or whole fish without any seasoning except salt and pepper, then serve it with this sauce.

> 1 cup chopped raisins
> 1 cup beef stock
> 1 cup dry white wine
> 1 tablespoon butter
> 1 tablespoon cornstarch
> Cold water
> 2 egg yolks, beaten
> Juice of 1 lemon
> 1 tablespoon chopped parsley

Simmer the raisins in the beef stock until they are soft. Add the wine and the butter and continue cooking over low heat until the butter melts. Add the cornstarch, dissolved in a little cold water, and cook, stirring constantly, until mixture is smooth. Stir a little cold water, about a tablespoon, into the beaten egg yolks; then carefully stir the egg mixture slowly into the sauce. Remove from heat. Blend in the lemon juice and the parsley. Pour over the cooked fish and serve. Makes about 2½ cups sauce.

Pescado Relleno
Stuffed Fish

Many Mexican recipes call for stuffed fish to be baked in banana leaves, but well-greased cooking parchment paper will do just as well. You can use crab meat instead of shrimp in this recipe, or mix the two if you like.

> ⅔ cup chopped cooked shrimp
> 1 small onion, minced
> 1 clove garlic, crushed
> 1 small green bell pepper, seeded and finely chopped
> 2 medium tomatoes, peeled and chopped

¼ cup dry white wine
1 teaspoon salt
½ teaspoon pepper
1 3-pound whole, boned bass, mackerel, pompano,
    or other firm white fish
Juice of 2 limes
2 tablespoons salt
Water
Juice of 2 oranges
1 teaspoon salt
½ teaspoon chili powder
4 tablespoons melted butter
Buttered parchment paper for baking
1 cup sliced fresh mushrooms, sautéed
Lemon wedges dipped in chopped parsley for garnish

Add the shrimp and the vegetables to the wine and blend
in the salt and pepper. Let the mixture stand for at least one hour.
Meanwhile, wash the whole, boned fish thoroughly and let it
soak for 10 or 15 minutes in the lime juice mixed with the salt
and enough water to completely cover. Remove fish from marinade; pat it dry with paper towels and brush the insides with the
orange juice. Next, rub the insides with the salt mixed with the
chili powder. Now, stuff the fish with the well-drained shrimp
mixture; close the opening with poultry pins and string. Cover
the bottom of a lightly-greased ovenproof glass baking pan with
a large sheet of the buttered parchment paper. Place the stuffed
fish on the paper, cover with the sautéed mushrooms, then bring
up all sides of the paper to make an airtight package and secure
with toothpicks. Or you can use two sheets of parchment paper;
one to cover the bottom of the baking pan and a top sheet, cut a
little larger, so that all four sides can be tucked under. Bake in a
preheated 375° F. oven for about 30 to 40 minutes. You can un-
wrap to test for doneness (when fish flakes easily with a fork).
When done, transfer fish to hot platter, remove pins and string,
and garnish with lemon wedges. Makes 6 servings.

Pescado Tampiqueño
Fish Tampico Style

This recipe is as tasty as it is easy.

2 pounds ocean fish fillets
Juice of one lime
Oil
Salt and pepper
¼ cup heavy cream
1 cup mayonnaise
1 tablespoon prepared mustard
1 cup sliced black olives
1 tablespoon chopped parsley

Brush the fillets on both sides with the lime juice and oil; then sprinkle with salt and pepper. Bake, uncovered, in a preheated 350° F. oven for about 20 minutes or until fish flakes easily with a fork. Transfer fillets to a hot platter. Mix the cream with the mayonnaise and mustard; stir in the olives and parsley, and spread the mixture on each fillet. Makes 4 servings.

Bacalao al Horno
Baked Cod

2 pounds fresh cod, cut into 1½-inch cubes
½ stick butter
2 small onions, cut into rings
1 clove garlic, chopped
2 teaspoons chili powder
¼ cup water
½ teaspoon salt
2 cups canned tomatoes, cut up
2 tablespoons melted butter
1 cup buttered bread crumbs

Rinse the fish and dry on paper towels. In a skillet, heat the butter and sauté the onion rings and garlic until tender and golden. Add the chili powder mixed with the ¼ cup water, the salt, and tomatoes and simmer for about 5 minutes until flavors are well blended. Pour the melted butter into a baking dish, arrange the pieces of fish in a single layer, pour on the tomato sauce, and sprinkle on the buttered bread crumbs. Bake in a pre-heated 350° F. oven for 25 to 30 minutes or until fish flakes easily with a fork. Makes 4 servings.

Bacalao en Salsa de Crema
Dried Cod in Cream Sauce

> 2 pounds dried, salted cod fillets
> Flour seasoned with salt and pepper
> ½ cup oil
> 2 medium onions, finely chopped
> 6 medium potatoes, boiled, peeled, and sliced
> 1 cup fish stock
> ¾ cup heavy cream
> ¼ cup sherry
> ¼ teaspoon nutmeg
> Dash cayenne pepper
> 2 tablespoons chopped parsley
> 3 hard-cooked eggs, quartered
> Pimiento strips

Desalt the cod by soaking in several changes of cool water for 6 to 8 hours or overnight. When ready to cook, drain the fish, cover with fresh cold water, bring to a simmer, and cook gently until the fish is tender and flakes easily with a fork. Drain the fillets, reserving the stock, and dry the fish on paper towels. Cut into slices across the grain and dust with the seasoned flour. In a skillet, heat the oil and fry the fish until lightly browned on both sides. Drain on paper towels and place in a greased casserole that has a cover. In the same oil, sauté the onions until tender and set aside; then sauté the sliced potatoes. Arrange the fried onions and potatoes over the fillets. Blend together the 1 cup of fish stock, cream, sherry, nutmeg, and cayenne and pour over the fish. Sprinkle with the parsley; then cover and cook for 30 minutes in a preheated 300° F. oven. Garnish with quartered eggs topped with pimiento strips. Makes 6 servings.

Guisado de Pescado
Fish Stew

3 tablespoons butter
2 medium onions, chopped
1 sweet red pepper, seeded and chopped
2 tablespoons minced parsley
1 canned green chili, seeded, rinsed, and chopped
¼ teaspoon black pepper
½ teaspoon nutmeg
3 pounds mixed fillets of sea bass, halibut, or whitefish
1 teaspoon salt
1½ cups white wine
2 cups water
1 dozen large cooked shrimp
1 7½-ounce can minced clams

In a large skillet that has a cover, heat the butter and sauté the onions, red pepper, parsley, and chili until onions are limp and vegetables are tender. Stir in the pepper and nutmeg. Cut the fish into serving-size pieces and arrange on top of the sautéed vegetables. Add salt, wine, and water. Cover the skillet and bring mixture to a boil; reduce heat and simmer for about 10 minutes. Add the shrimp and the clams with their liquor. Cook for another 5 minutes or until fish flakes easily with a fork. Makes 6 to 8 generous portions.

Paella

There are countless versions of this marvelous dish of herbed rice combined with pork, chicken, and shellfish. It is said to have been brought to Spain by the Moors and quickly adopted by all Mediterranean countries. Inventive Mexican cooks will vary the basic recipe to suit their own tastes, and you can jolly well do the same. Paella makes a great buffet supper dish, served with a green salad and hot buttered French bread.

¼ cup olive or salad oil
2 medium onions, chopped
1 clove garlic, minced
2 cups long grain white rice
½ teaspoon saffron
3 cups hot chicken broth
4 slices bacon, partially cooked and cut into small strips*
1 16-ounce can (No. 303) tomatoes
1 2-ounce jar pimientos, sliced
¼ cup chopped green bell pepper
1 pound halibut, red snapper, or mahimahi, cut into bite-size chunks
1 pound shrimp, cooked, peeled, and deveined
1 teaspoon salt
½ teaspoon orégano
½ teaspoon tarragon
3 whole chicken breasts, cut in half, browned and cooked
6 raw shrimp, shelled and deveined
12 raw cherrystone or littleneck clams in the shells

Heat the oil in a large kettle or Dutch oven and sauté the onions and garlic until limp; push to one side. In the same kettle, sauté the rice until lightly browned. Dissolve the saffron in the hot chicken broth; add to the rice mixture. Then add the bacon strips, tomatoes, pimientos, bell pepper, fish, shrimp, and seasonings; mix well. Cover, bring just to a boil, reduce heat, and simmer for 20 minutes. Meanwhile, thoroughly rinse and scrub the clams and, in a separate saucepan, steam them until their shells have popped open. Remove clams and arrange them with the raw shrimp around the rice. Place chicken breasts on top of rice. Cover and again simmer for about 20 minutes or until shrimp are done. Makes 6 servings.

* Four pork sausage links, sliced, or two 4-inch chorizo sausage links, skinned and crumbled, may be substituted for the bacon. For variety, add one or more of the following ingredients during the last 10 minutes of cooking: 1 package frozen peas; 1 package frozen green beans; 1 can artichoke hearts, rinsed and drained.

Señor Pico Gulf Shrimp Devine

⅔ cup olive oil
⅓ cup lemon juice
½ teaspoon salt
⅛ teaspoon pepper
2 pounds raw shrimp, shelled and deveined
3 tablespoons butter
1 clove garlic, crushed
1 cup blanched, slivered almonds
Dash Tabasco sauce
½ cup dry vermouth

Make marinade of olive oil, lemon juice, and seasonings and marinate shrimp for at least 2 hours (overnight will do no harm). Melt butter in large skillet; add garlic and drained shrimp, reserving marinade for later. Stir-fry shrimp over medium heat until they are pink. Discard garlic; remove shrimp to a hot platter. Sauté slivered almonds in butter until golden; then add the marinade, Tabasco, and vermouth. When well blended, pour sauce over shrimp. Serve with saffron rice mixed with chopped chives or finely chopped green onions. Makes 4 servings.

Camarones en Escabeche
Pickled Shrimp

A tasty addition for your party buffets.

2 pounds raw shrimp, unshelled
1 large onion, sliced
3 cloves garlic, crushed
½ cup oil

MARINADE

½ cup salad oil
½ cup wine vinegar
Juice from 1 3½-ounce can jalapeño chilies
½ teaspoon dry mustard
Salt and pepper to taste

GARNISH

3 large onions, peeled, sliced, and soaked in lemon juice
Jalapeño chilies (from can) cut into strips
3 large tomatoes, peeled and sliced

Shell and devein the shrimp and wash them well. Gently sauté the onion and the garlic in the oil; then add the shrimp and stir-fry until they turn pink. Remove shrimp from pan, drain on paper towels, and let cool.

Meanwhile, make the following marinade while the onion slices for the garnish are soaking in lemon juice. Mix the oil and vinegar, add the juice from the canned jalapeños, the mustard, salt, and pepper. Blend the mixture thoroughly. Add the cooled shrimp and let chill.

When ready to serve, drain the shrimp and garnish with the slices of drained onions, tomatoes, and the jalapeño strips.

1. Festive Mexican Party Table

2. Mexican Drinks: Sangría; Durango; Potted Parrot; Margarita cocktail; Señor Pico Tequila Daiquiri (from left to right, top and bottom)

3. Enchiladas with Green Sauce and Sour Cream

4. Red Snapper Veracruz Style

5. Paella

Camarones en Panisados
Shrimp Fritters

1⅓ cups sifted all-purpose flour
1½ teaspoons baking powder
¼ teaspoon salt
Dash cayenne pepper
¼ teaspoon ginger
Dash cinnamon
⅔ cup milk
1 egg, well beaten
1½ cups cooked shrimp, coarsely chopped

Sift together the dry ingredients; blend milk and egg and add slowly to the dry ingredients, a little at a time. Stir in the shrimp. Drop mixture from a tablespoon into deep hot fat (375° F.) Fry for about 3 minutes or until golden brown. Drain on paper towels. Serve at once. Makes 4 to 6 servings.

Jaibas Rellenas
Stuffed Crab

Meat of 8 medium-size crabs (about 2 cups), reserve
  shells
2 tablespoons butter
2 tablespoons minced onion
1½ cups canned tomatoes, chopped
1 pimiento, chopped
10 pitted green olives, sliced
¼ cup ground almonds
½ cup bread crumbs
1 teaspoon prepared mustard
2 drops Tabasco sauce or to taste
Salt and pepper to taste

2 hard-cooked eggs, chopped
¼ cup bread crumbs
2 tablespoons butter

Remove claws from crabs and cut off the tops of the shells. When all the crab meat is removed, thoroughly clean the shells for use as serving containers. Finely chop all the crab meat.

In a large skillet, heat the butter and sauté the onion until limp and golden. Add the tomatoes, pimiento, olives, ground almonds, half of the bread crumbs, and seasonings. Cook slowly, stirring frequently, until mixture is well thickened. Stir in the hard-cooked eggs and the crab meat and distribute the mixture into the crab shells. Sprinkle the tops with the remaining bread crumbs, dot with butter, and place stuffed shells under broiler just long enough to brown. Makes 8 servings.

NOTE: If you want to use already-shelled crab meat, you can substitute individual ramekins or scallop shells for the crab shells.

Ostiones en Cazuela
Oyster Casserole

3 dozen oysters
Juice of 3 limes
½ teaspoon salt
⅓ cup bread crumbs
¼ teaspoon each salt, pepper, and orégano
2 tablespoons butter
2 tablespoons chopped onions
1 tablespoon minced parsley
2 cups canned tomatoes, chopped
Dash of Tabasco
4 eggs, separated
Cayenne pepper

Bread crumbs for topping
Butter for topping

Drain the oysters and marinate in the lime juice with the salt. Mix the bread crumbs with the salt, pepper, and orégano and set aside. Heat the butter in a skillet and sauté the onions until tender and golden. Add the parsley, tomatoes, and Tabasco and cook gently for a few minutes to blend the flavors. Beat the egg whites until stiff but not dry; add the yolks, one at a time, beating constantly. In a large, well-buttered casserole, alternate layers of drained oysters, the tomato mixture, the beaten eggs, and the seasoned bread crumbs. Top with a layer of bread crumbs, dust sparingly with cayenne pepper, and dot with butter. Bake in a preheated 350° F. oven for about 20 minutes or until mixture is hot and the topping is brown. Makes 6 servings.

Ostiones a la Española
Spanish Oysters

3 dozen oysters in shells
½ stick butter
1 teaspoon finely chopped onions
1 tablespoon flour
¼ cup chicken stock
¼ cup sherry
3 egg yolks, beaten
Salt and pepper to taste
3 tablespoons dry bread crumbs
Butter

Remove oysters from shells; thoroughly clean the shells and set aside. Heat the ½ stick of butter and sauté the onions until tender. Stir in the flour and cook gently for a few minutes. Add the stock and wine; cook until thick, stirring constantly. Remove from heat and, when slightly cooled, thoroughly mix in the beaten egg yolks, the salt and pepper, and then the oysters. Distribute the oysters and sauce into the shells; sprinkle on the bread crumbs and dot with butter. Place oysters on a large cookie sheet and bake in a preheated 400° F. oven for a few minutes or until sauce is bubbly and topping is brown. Makes 6 servings.

Señor Pico Spaghetti Las Cruces

> 1 8-ounce can whole clams
> 1 8-ounce can minced clams
> 1 8-ounce can shrimp
> 1 8-ounce can Dungeness crab (optional)
> 2 tablespoons butter
> 1 medium-sized onion, chopped
> 1 clove garlic, mashed
> ½ cup dry white wine
> 1 stick butter
> 3 dashes Tabasco
> Freshly ground pepper to taste
> 1 cup (1 can) white sauce
> 1 pound spaghetti
> Grated Parmesan cheese
> Chopped chives (optional)

Open the cans but do not drain any of them. In a skillet, heat the butter and sauté the onion and garlic until limp and tender. Still over low heat, add the cans of shellfish with their liquor, the wine, and the butter; stir all together and cook until the butter is completely melted. Stir in the Tabasco, pepper and white sauce. There should be enough salt in the canned seafood, but you can add more if you want. Keep the sauce warm over low heat, stirring occasionally. In the meantime, cook the spaghetti according to package instructions, just until *al dente* (with a slight resistance to the bite). Drain the spaghetti, place it on a large, deep platter, and pour on all the sauce, but don't mix it through until you serve it. Sprinkle on a generous amount of Parmesan cheese and then top with chopped chives. Makes 6 to 8 servings, depending on size of appetites.

Pulpos Borrachos
Drunken Squid

Many Americans shudder at the thought of eating squid, and yet the meat is delicate and much sweeter than lobster, to say nothing of much less trouble to prepare.

Squid is a favorite dish in Mexico, just as it is in the Mediterranean countries, the Orient, and in the Pacific islands. I ate this dish at a friend's home in Yucatán and he served it with rice. Believe me, we all cleaned our plates.

    2 pounds cleaned squid meat
    ½ cup brandy
    1 teaspoon salt
    2 tablespoons butter
    1 large onion, chopped
    1 clove garlic, minced
    2 tablespoons chopped parsley
    4 cups canned tomato sauce
    1 cup dry white wine
    Salt and pepper to taste
    Pitted black olives for garnish
    Enough cooked rice for 6 servings

Cut the squid into cubes and marinate it for about an hour in the brandy and salt. Place squid and marinade in a saucepan, adding just enough water to the marinade to cover the squid, and boil gently until fork-tender. Remove squid from the saucepan and set aside, saving the broth for later use. In a large skillet, heat the butter and sauté the onion and garlic until

133

limp and tender. Add the parsley and tomato sauce and cook for another 4 or 5 minutes until flavors are well blended. Add the squid, the reserved brandy-broth, the wine, salt, and pepper to the tomato mixture and continue to simmer for another 30 minutes. Serve with rice and garnish with pitted black olives. Makes 6 servings.

Aves
(Poultry)

I'll wager there are more chickens throughout the world than any other kind of "meat." In Mexico, where poultry is plentiful and well loved, they have developed all kinds of wonderful chicken dishes. Many of these recipes originated from French, Austrian, and Italian influences. Then, of course, the Mexicans added their own inimitable touches. So now on to these good chicken dishes.

Señor Pico Chicken

> 2 2- to 2¼-pound fryers
> Salt and pepper to taste
> 1 teaspoon monosodium glutamate
> 4 thick slices Monterey Jack cheese
> Flour for coating
> 2 eggs beaten with ¼ cup water
> Bread crumbs
> Oil
> 2 carrots, finely diced
> 2 stalks celery, chopped
> ½ cup chopped onions
> ½ cup white wine
> ½ cup chicken stock
> Sauce for Señor Pico Chicken (recipe follows)

Split chickens, crack backbones, and remove ribs. Season with salt, pepper, and monosodium glutamate. Place one piece of Monterey Jack cheese on half of each chicken half and fold over; skewer or tie together with string. Dust chickens with flour, dip in egg wash and then in crumbs. Sauté in hot oil in large skillet, turning frequently so chickens brown evenly. When browned, remove to roasting pan or large casserole. In the same skillet, sauté the carrots, celery, and onions until tender. Add to chicken in roasting pan. Wash out skillet with wine and stock and add to chicken. Cover and bake in a preheated 350° F. oven for about 30 minutes or until tender. Remove chicken to heated serving platter and keep warm in oven. Make sauce in roasting pan, using drippings and vegetables. Makes 4 servings.

SAUCE FOR SEÑOR PICO CHICKEN

> 1 tablespoon Dijon mustard
> 1 small can tomato sauce
> ½ teaspoon salt

¼ teaspoon pepper
½ teaspoon Worcestershire sauce
½ cup white wine
About 2½ cups chicken broth
2 tablespoons cornstarch mixed with ¼ cup cold water

Sieve vegetables left in roasting pan, then return to pan. Add mustard, tomato sauce, seasonings, and wine. Stir well and add enough chicken broth to make 4 cups of liquid. Thicken with cornstarch mixture. Simmer for a few moments, stirring constantly, and pour over chicken.

Rajas de Chili con Pollo
Creamed Chicken with Chilies

Rajas is the Mexican word given to strips of green poblano chilies, and *pollo* means chicken. Put them together and you have a delicious concoction that is particularly good for buffet suppers. If canned poblano chilies are not available, you can substitute bell peppers. Parboil and then julienne them. Keep the rest of the menu light. A good cold California Gewürztraminer would go well with this.

1 4- to 5-pound capon, cleaned
2 teaspoons salt
1 teaspoon monosodium glutamate
1 cup finely chopped onions
1 cup melted butter
1 cup flour
1 quart whipping cream
6 corn tortillas made into tostadas, or
   1 small package tortilla chips
3 canned poblano chilies, seeded, rinsed, and julienned
Oil
½ pound Cheddar cheese, grated

Simmer capon in boiling water until tender, adding salt and monosodium glutamate when about half done. Cool, skin, and bone. Cut meat into ¾-inch chunks. Using the top of a double boiler over direct heat, sauté the chopped onions in the melted butter until they are limp and transparent. Add flour and stir thoroughly; place pan over hot water and gradually stir in the whipping cream. Continue stirring until mixture comes to a boil and is smooth. Reduce heat and let simmer gently, stirring now and then to prevent scorching. If mixture seems too thick, it can be thinned with a little of the chicken broth. Meanwhile, cut tortillas into triangles and fry in oil to a golden brown. Add chicken meat to cream sauce and stir in chili strips; mix thoroughly. In a greased 4-quart casserole, alternate layers of tostadas, creamed chicken, and cheese, saving enough cheese for a thick layer on top. Bake in a preheated 375° F. oven for 30 to 45 minutes, or until bubbling and cheese has melted. Makes 6 servings.

Pollo Envinado
Chicken in Wine Sauce

> 1 4½- to 5-pound chicken, cut into serving pieces
> 4 cups seasoned boiling water*
> Flour seasoned with salt and pepper
> ½ cup oil
> 1 small onion, chopped
> 1 teaspoon saffron
> ½ teaspoon nutmeg
> Salt and pepper to taste
> 1 teaspoon orégano
> 1 teaspoon mint
> 1 cup white wine
> 1 cup chicken stock
> 1½ tablespoons flour
> 3 tablespoons water

Place the chicken pieces in a kettle, cover with the seasoned boiling water, and simmer, covered, until tender. Remove chicken from stock and pat dry. Strain the stock and set aside. Roll the dried chicken pieces in the seasoned flour and fry gently in the oil until brown. Add the chopped onion and when it is golden add the spices, herbs, wine, and stock. Thicken the mixture with a *roux* made by mixing the flour and water; stir until sauce is thickened and smooth. Makes 6 servings.

* Season the water as for soups with an onion, some celery tops, parsley, a carrot, salt, and pepper.

Arroz con Pollo
Chicken with Rice

> ¼ cup oil
> 1 3½- to 4-pound chicken, cut into serving pieces
> ½ cup chopped onions
> 1 clove garlic, minced
> 1 cup long grain white rice
> 2 tomatoes, peeled and chopped
> ¼ teaspoon saffron
> 2 cups hot chicken broth
> 1 teaspoon salt
> 1 teaspoon chili powder
> 1 2-ounce jar pimientos

In a large skillet with a cover, heat the oil and lightly brown the chicken pieces; remove chicken and set aside. In the same oil, sauté the onions and garlic until golden and limp. Add the rice and sauté until golden. Add the tomatoes; then mix the saffron with the chicken broth and add along with the rest of the ingredients. Stir well to blend. Add chicken pieces, cover tightly, and simmer slowly over low heat for 30 to 40 minutes, or until chicken is tender and rice has absorbed the liquid. Makes 4 servings.

Pollo Borracho
Mexican Chicken Drunken Style

    5 whole chicken breasts, split in half
    Flour
    Salt and pepper
    ½ cup oil
    1 onion, finely chopped
    1 teaspoon chopped parsley
    1½ cups canned tomatoes
    ½ cup blanched almonds
    ¾ cup chopped cooked ham (optional)
    ¼ cup raisins
    ¼ teaspoon clove
    ¼ teaspoon cinnamon
    ¼ teaspoon pepper
    ⅛ teaspoon nutmeg
    1 cup dry sherry

Roll the chicken breasts in flour seasoned with salt and pepper. Sauté them in the oil until lightly browned on both sides; remove from skillet and set aside. In the same skillet, sauté the finely chopped onion until just tender. Add parsley and tomatoes and simmer for a few minutes. Meanwhile, grind half of the almonds (use a blender), and coarsely chop the remainder; add both to the skillet along with all the rest of the ingredients and simmer over moderate heat for a few minutes. Place the browned chicken breasts in a casserole and pour on the contents of the skillet. Cover and bake for about 45 minutes in a preheated 325° F. oven. Makes 10 servings.

NOTE: This dish can be made ahead of time—even the day before. Just refrigerate and reheat. Or it can be frozen until needed.

Pollo en Vino Tinto
Chicken in Red Wine

½ cup oil or butter
2 frying chickens, cut into serving pieces
3 yellow squash, sliced
1 large onion, sliced
½ clove garlic, minced
3 tomatoes, sliced
1 teaspoon salt
¼ teaspoon ground pepper
1 bay leaf
¼ teaspoon fines herbes
1 2-inch stick cinnamon
3 whole cloves
1 cup chicken broth
1 cup dry red wine
1 large can whole kernel corn, drained

Heat the oil or butter in a skillet and lightly brown the chicken pieces; then transfer them to a Dutch oven or baking dish. In the same skillet, sauté the squash and set aside; then sauté the onion and garlic until limp. Add the tomatoes and cook until mushy. Add seasonings, chicken broth, and wine and bring to a boil. Add squash and pour entire mixture over chicken. Spoon the drained corn over the top. Cover and bake in a preheated 350° F. oven for about 1 hour or until chicken is tender. Baste occasionally with liquid, adding more chicken broth if necessary. Before serving, remove cinnamon stick, cloves, and bay leaf. Serve with steamed rice. Makes 4 to 5 servings, depending upon size of chickens.

Pollo con Nuez en Salsa Verde
Green Chicken with Walnuts

1 3½- to 4-pound fryer, cut into serving pieces
2 tablespoons olive oil
2 tablespoons butter
1 large onion finely chopped
1 clove garlic, chopped
1 cup chicken stock
1 cup dry white wine
Salt and pepper to taste
1 cup walnuts
1 10-ounce can Mexican green tomatoes, drained
  and cut up
2 small green bell peppers, seeded and cut up*
½ cup chopped parsley

In a large skillet, sauté the chicken pieces in the heated oil and butter until they are golden; then transfer them to a flame-proof casserole that has a cover. Sauté the onion and the garlic in the oil remaining in the pan until the onion is limp and golden. Add to the casserole with the chicken stock, wine, salt and pepper to taste; cook over very low heat, covered, for about 1 hour or until the chicken is tender. Grind the walnuts very fine in an electric blender; add the drained green tomatoes, peppers and parsley and blend for a few seconds more. Add the blended mixture to the casserole and simmer gently for 5 minutes until the sauce has thickened to medium consistency; thin, if necessary, with a little of the liquid from the canned tomatoes or a little more wine. Makes 6 servings.

* One canned poblano chili may be substituted for the green peppers. Be sure to seed and rinse it before using.

Pollo con Hongos
Chicken with Mushrooms

    4 tablespoons oil
    1 3½- to 4-pound chicken, cut into serving pieces
    1 pound fresh mushrooms, sliced
    1 medium onion, chopped
    1 clove garlic, chopped
    1 cup canned tomatoes, drained and chopped
    1 tablespoon chopped parsley
    Salt and pepper to taste
    1 teaspoon sugar
    2 teaspoons chili powder
    1 cup chicken stock
    ½ cup evaporated milk

Heat the oil in a skillet, and sauté the chicken pieces until golden. Transfer to a casserole that has a cover. Sauté the mushrooms, onion, and garlic in the remaining oil until tender. Add the tomatoes and seasonings and cook for a few minutes until flavors are blended. Stir in the chicken stock and pour the mixture over the chicken pieces. Cover the casserole and bake in a preheated 350° F. oven for about 45 minutes to 1 hour, or until chicken is tender. Just before serving, stir in the evaporated milk and heat through, without letting the sauce come to a boil. Makes 6 servings.

Pollo Verde con Ajonjolí
Green Chicken with Sesame Seeds

    1 3½- to 4-pound chicken, cut into serving pieces
    1½ cups chicken stock
    ½ cup dry white wine
    1 cup sesame seeds

1 onion, chopped
1 clove garlic, chopped
5 or 6 sprigs of parsley
2 10-ounce cans Mexican green tomatoes
1 or 2 canned poblano chilies, seeded, rinsed, and
　　cut up
2 tablespoons oil
Salt and pepper to taste

Place the chicken pieces in a poaching pan with the stock and wine; cover and simmer for 35 to 45 minutes or until almost tender. Drain, reserving the stock, and transfer the chicken to a covered casserole; keep warm. In a blender, grind the sesame seeds until they are pulverized, and set aside. Now, in the blender, place the onion, garlic, parsley, drained tomatoes (reserving the liquid), and the chilies and blend to a coarse purée. Heat the oil in a skillet; add the purée and the sesame seeds, and cook for about 4 or 5 minutes, stirring constantly. Add the liquid from the canned tomatoes and as much as necessary of the chicken stock to make the sauce medium-thick. Add salt and pepper to taste. Pour the sauce over the chicken in the casserole, cover, and bake in a preheated 350° F. oven for 20 to 30 minutes or until the chicken is tender. Makes 6 servings.

Pollo Mexicana
Chicken Mexican Style

1 4½- to 5-pound roasting chicken, cut into
　　serving pieces
Juice of 1 lime, or juice of ½ large lemon
1 tablespoon salt
¼ cup oil
3 medium onions, chopped
3 cloves garlic, minced

6. Señor Pico Beef Brochette Yucatán

7. Matambre

8. Ensalada Chalupa Compuesta (Tortilla Sandwich Salad)

9. Molded Avocado Ring with Sour Cream Shrimp Dressing

2½ cups (No. 2 can) tomatoes, drained and chopped
2 tablespoons seedless raisins
2 tablespoons prunes, pitted and chopped
½ cup julienned, cooked ham
2 tablespoons butter
Freshly ground pepper to taste
½ teaspoon cinnamon
1½ cups chicken broth
½ cup almonds, slivered
2 tablespoons pimiento-stuffed olives, sliced

Brush the chicken pieces with the lime or lemon juice and sprinkle with salt. In a very large skillet, heat the oil and sauté the chicken until golden brown. Add all other ingredients except broth, almonds, and olives. Sauté for about 10 minutes, turning frequently. Add the chicken broth, cover, and simmer over low heat for about 1 hour or until chicken is tender. Add more chicken broth or wine if sauce appears too scant. Transfer chicken pieces to a heated platter, pour on the sauce and garnish with the almonds and olives. Makes 6 servings.

Guisado de Pollo
Chicken Stew

2 tablespoons butter
2 tablespoons oil
2 2½-pound fryers, cut into serving pieces
1 cup canned tomatoes, chopped
2 medium onions, chopped
1 clove garlic, chopped
1½ cups coarsely chopped cooked ham
1 bay leaf
½ teaspoon thyme
½ teaspoon marjoram

2 canned green chilies, seeded, rinsed, and chopped
1 tablespoon lemon juice
1½ cups dry white wine
Salt and pepper to taste

In a large skillet that has a cover, heat the butter and oil, and sauté the chicken pieces until golden. Add the remaining ingredients. Cook, covered, over low heat for about 1 hour or until the chicken is tender. Makes 6 servings.

Pollo Frito
Fried Chicken

1 3- to 3½-pound fryer, cut into serving pieces
½ cup flour
1 teaspoon each salt and paprika
⅛ teaspoon pepper
2 tablespoons each oil and butter
1 small onion, chopped
1 clove garlic, chopped
2 tablespoons chopped parsley
1 green bell pepper, chopped
3 tablespoons flour
1 cup chicken stock
Salt and pepper to taste
1 tablespoon lemon juice

Roll the chicken pieces in the flour, which has been well mixed with the seasonings. Heat the oil and butter in a skillet; place chicken pieces skin side down in skillet and cook, uncovered, for 15 to 25 minutes on each side, turning only once. Transfer chicken to heated serving platter and keep warm. In the same skillet, adding more butter if necessary, sauté the onion, garlic, parsley, and pepper. Push the vegetables to one side, stir in the 3 tablespoons of flour, cooking slowly for a few minutes; then add the chicken stock and stir until thickened. Add salt and pepper to taste and lemon juice; blend well. Pour this sauce over the chicken and serve. Makes 4 servings.

Pollo con Naranjas
Chicken in Orange Juice

2 2½-pound fryers, cut into serving pieces
Flour seasoned with salt and pepper
¼ cup oil
1 cup fresh orange juice, strained
1 cup chicken broth
1 cup dry white wine
½ cup seedless raisins
½ cup crushed pineapple, drained
½ teaspoon cinnamon
¼ teaspoon ground cloves
Dash cayenne pepper
¼ cup slivered almonds, toasted

Roll the chicken in the seasoned flour. Heat the oil in a flameproof casserole that has a cover and lightly brown the chicken on both sides. Combine the rest of the ingredients, except the toasted almonds, in a saucepan and cook for a few minutes over moderate heat to blend flavors. Pour the heated sauce over the chicken and bake in a preheated 350° F. oven for about 35 minutes or until chicken is tender. Transfer chicken pieces to a heated serving platter. Thicken the gravy, if desired, with a *roux* made of 2 parts water to 1 part flour. Mix the roux into the gravy and cook on top of the stove, stirring constantly, until thickened. Pour gravy over chicken and sprinkle on the toasted almonds. Makes 6 servings.

Pollo con Frutas
Chicken with Fruits

    1 3½- to 4-pound chicken
    Boiling water
    1 teaspoon salt
    2 teaspoons chili powder
    ½ teaspoon freshly ground pepper
    2 tablespoons finely minced onions
    2 tablespoons butter
    2 tablespoons oil
    1 cup tomato juice
    1 unpeeled red apple, cored and thinly sliced
    Sugar
    1 peeled orange, thinly sliced
    Avocado slices for garnish
    Seedless white grapes for garnish

Place the chicken pieces close together in a kettle and add only enough boiling water to cover. Stir in the salt, chili powder, pepper and onions, and simmer slowly for 45 minutes. Remove chicken from broth and pat dry on paper towels.

Heat the butter and oil in a skillet, and gently brown the chicken pieces on all sides; then transfer them to a shallow baking-serving dish. Add the tomato juice to the broth, heat to boiling, and pour the broth over the chicken. Cover with the apple slices sprinkled with sugar, alternating with the orange slices. Bake in a preheated 350° F. oven for about 20 minutes or until apples are tender. Just before serving, edge the dish with a garnish of avocado slices alternating with grapes. (Halved Malaga grapes, when in season, are especially nice to use.) Makes 4 to 5 servings.

Pollo con Chavacanos
Chicken with Apricots

½ pound dried apricots
½ stick butter
2 2½-pound fryers, cut into serving pieces
1 large onion, finely chopped
1 clove garlic, chopped
2 cups chopped canned tomatoes, drained
1 cup chicken stock
1 teaspoon chili powder
Salt and pepper to taste
½ cup dry sherry

Place apricots in a saucepan; add water to a depth of ½ inch above the fruit. Bring to a boil, uncovered. Simmer gently for 20 to 30 minutes or until apricots are tender and plump. Meanwhile, heat the butter in a skillet that has a cover and lightly brown the chicken pieces. Add the onion and garlic and sauté until tender. Then add the chopped tomatoes and stir to blend flavors. Drain the apricots and chop them coarsely; add to the skillet with the chicken stock. Season with chili powder, salt, and pepper; cover; and simmer gently for about 1 hour, or until the chicken is tender. When chicken is done, add the sherry and cook for just a few more minutes before serving. Makes 6 servings.

Mole Poblano de Pavo
Turkey in Chili Sauce, Puebla Style

The Spanish word *mole* (pronounced "molay") means a sauce made with chilies. While there are many mole recipes, the most famous is the Mole Poblano, the chili sauce made with bitter chocolate and traditionally served with turkey for many festive occasions.

149

One of several legends has it that this sauce originated during early colonial times and was invented by the nuns in the Santa Rosa convent of Puebla. It seems the good sisters had a surprise visit from a viceroy and an archbishop and felt that they must come up with a feast worthy of these VIPs. While the turkey was cooking, they proceeded to improve on their basic chili sauce recipe by adding everything but the kitchen sink. The result was a smash hit and a sauce that has remained a national favorite to this day.

Don't let the use of chocolate in this recipe turn you off. In Mexico, the people use chocolate in sauces for damn near everything, including beef tongue and enchiladas. It's great.

1 8- to 9-pound turkey, disjointed and cut into
   serving pieces
Cold water
2 teaspoons salt
6 dried ancho chilies
4 dried pasilla chilies
4 dried mulato chilies
4 tablespoons lard*
1 cup coarsely chopped onions
2 cloves garlic, chopped
½ teaspoon anise seeds
2 tablespoons sesame seeds
3 sprigs Chinese parsley
1 tortilla, broken into small pieces
3 medium tomatoes, peeled, seeded, and chopped
1 cup blanched almonds
½ cup seedless raisins
½ teaspoon ground cloves

1 teaspoon cinnamon
½ teaspoon coriander seeds, ground
1½ 1-ounce squares unsweetened chocolate
1 teaspoon salt
¼ teaspoon freshly ground pepper

Place the turkey pieces in a large kettle; cover with cold water, add the salt, and bring to a boil over high heat. Reduce heat to low, cover the kettle, and simmer for 1 hour. Meanwhile, prepare the chilies as described in chapter on chilies and set aside.

Now remove the turkey pieces, reserving 2 cups of the stock, and pat them thoroughly dry with paper towels. Heat the lard in a skillet and brown the turkey pieces on all sides, turning them frequently. When thoroughly browned, transfer them to a flameproof casserole that has a cover. Leave the remaining lard in the skillet for later use.

Combine the prepared chilies, onions, garlic, anise and sesame seeds, parsley, tortilla pieces, tomatoes, nuts, raisins, cloves, cinnamon and ground coriander seeds. Blend, a portion at a time if necessary, in an electric blender until coarsely puréed. Reheat the lard in the skillet, adding more if necessary to make 3 tablespoons. Pour the mole into the hot lard and simmer it, stirring constantly, for about 5 minutes. Add the 2 cups of stock, the chocolate, salt, and pepper, and continue to cook over low heat, stirring frequently, until the chocolate has melted. The sauce should be quite thick. Pour the sauce over the turkey in the casserole, turning each piece until thoroughly coated, and cook, covered, over very low heat for 30 minutes.

To serve, arrange the turkey pieces on a heated platter, ladle on the sauce, and sprinkle on the 2 tablespoons of sesame seeds. Makes 8 to 10 servings.

* Lard imparts a traditional flavor to this dish, but oil may be substituted.

Pavo Relleno No. 1
Turkey with Stuffing

FOR AN 8-POUND TURKEY:

2 tablespoons lard or oil
1 onion, finely chopped
1 clove garlic, chopped
2 pounds ground lean pork
1 tart apple, peeled, cored, and chopped
1 large, firm banana, peeled and sliced
¼ cup raisins
½ cup pine nuts
1 canned green chili, seeded, rinsed, and chopped
2 medium tomatoes, peeled and chopped
Salt and pepper to taste
Melted butter
Flour for thickening gravy
Chicken stock
Dry white wine
Salt and pepper to taste

In a large skillet, heat the lard or oil and sauté the onion and garlic until tender and limp. Add the pork and fry, stirring constantly, until browned. Stir in the fruits, nuts, and chili, and cook for a few minutes to blend. Drain off any excess fat; then stir in the tomatoes and salt and pepper. Continue cooking for another few minutes. Let mixture cool; then stuff it into the turkey.

Brush the turkey with melted butter and place it, breast side up, on a rack in a roasting pan. Roast in a preheated 325° F. oven for about 2½ hours or until turkey is done. Baste several times during cooking with pan drippings or melted butter.

Make gravy, using just enough flour to thicken the pan drippings; add chicken stock mixed with wine. Season to taste with salt and pepper. Makes 6 to 8 servings.

Pavo Relleno No. 2
Turkey with Stuffing

If the typically Mexican turkey stuffing is a little much for your taste buds, try this recipe from one of my good friends, who is a cook par excellence. Her recipe is based on a traditionally American stuffing with interesting overtones of Mexicana. In short, the best of both worlds.

FOR A 15-POUND TURKEY:

1 cup (½ pound) butter
6 cups soft white bread crumbs
6 cups corn bread crumbs
1 cup chopped celery
½ cup chopped onions
6 cups tamales (about 12), broken in pieces
2 teaspoons salt
½ teaspoon pepper
1 teaspoon orégano
1 tablespoon chili powder
2 to 2½ cups turkey broth*

In a very large skillet, heat the butter and sauté the crumbs and chopped vegetables, stirring constantly, until the vegetables are tender. Add tamales and seasonings; then moisten with the broth. (Slightly more broth may be needed, depending on the dryness of the crumbs, but do not make the mixture too wet or the dressing will be soggy.) Let the mixture cool thoroughly, then stuff the bird lightly, and do not pack the dressing. Roast according to your favorite method. Makes about 12 servings.

* Broth is made by boiling the wing tips, neck, and giblets of the turkey. As a substitute, chicken bouillon may be used.

Pavo con Mole Poblanos y Queso
Turkey with Peppers and Cheese

Leftover turkey? Here's a tasty way to serve it.

4 green bell peppers
½ stick butter
4 onions, chopped
3 cups cooked turkey, cut into cubes
½ pint sour cream
Salt and freshly ground pepper to taste
⅛ teaspoon marjoram
⅛ teaspoon thyme
1 cup grated mild Cheddar cheese
Parsley for garnish
Paprika for garnish

Wash the peppers, cut in half, and remove stems and seeds. Place the peppers in a saucepan, cover with lightly salted water, and parboil them, covered, for about 5 minutes. Remove peppers from pan, drain them, and cut them into 1-inch squares. In a large skillet, heat the butter and sauté the chopped onions and pepper pieces. When tender, add the cubed turkey, sour cream, salt, pepper, marjoram, and thyme. Simmer until heated through but do not allow the mixture to boil. When hot, top with cheese, parsley, and paprika, and when the cheese melts, serve at once. Makes 6 servings.

Conejo Mexicana
Rabbit Mexican Style

2 1- to 1½-pound rabbits
½ cup peanut oil
2 small chili peppers

2 cloves garlic, crushed
Flour
Sauce for Conejo Mexicana (recipe follows)

Have your butcher cut legs from rabbits and cut backs into three pieces. Preheat heavy kettle, add oil, and heat. Drop in chili peppers and let them fry until brown, pressing them occasionally with a fork to extract the pepper juice, then discard. Rub each piece of rabbit with the crushed garlic, then flour lightly and sauté pieces in the chili-flavored oil. When golden brown, remove from kettle and place in a large covered baking dish. Keep warm in oven at very low heat while the sauce is being prepared.

SAUCE FOR CONEJO MEXICANA

⅓ stick butter
1 large carrot, finely diced
½ cup finely chopped onions
3 tablespoons chopped green pepper
1 cup chopped mushrooms
2 tablespoons flour
2 cups chicken broth
Juice of 1 small orange
1 heaping tablespoon peanut butter
½ teaspoon cuminseeds
1 tablespoon toasted sesame seeds
3 cloves
3 slices orange peel
Dash nutmeg
Salt and pepper to taste
1 tablespoon chopped parsley

Pour off the oil in which the rabbit was cooked and heat the butter in the kettle. When hot, add the carrots, onions, green pepper, and mushrooms. Sauté over very low heat, stirring frequently, until tender. Be careful not to let brown. Add the flour and mix well with the vegetables, then add the broth and stir until slightly thickened. Add all of the rest of the ingredients except the parsley. Let mixture simmer for about 10 minutes until thoroughly blended. Sprinkle the rabbit in the casserole with salt and pour the cooked sauce over it. Sprinkle with parsley, cover, and bake in a preheated 350° F. oven for about 1 hour, or until tender. Baked potatoes go well with this dish. Makes 6 servings.

Carnes
[Meats]

Have you ever seen a meat market in the Mexican country-side? *Eyi, eyi, eyi, eyi, eyi!* It can be awfully icky, yet the peasants don't seem to suffer any ill effects. Maybe, it's because in the hinterlands, the meat is always boiled, just as it has been for centuries.

Even in the metropolitan areas of Mexico, where markets are modern and refrigeration prevails, you will find a great many Mexican dishes that call for preboiling the meat—even such tender cuts as we would fry, broil, or roast. Possibly this cooking method has survived from the days before the Spanish introduced oil, lard, and butter to the country. In many instances, the cuts of

157

meat are quite different from what you find in our markets—and as for frozen meats, forget it. The Mexicans simply don't like them. They want fresh meat and that's what their markets supply for them.

Beef, pork, lamb, and veal are as popular in Mexico as they are in the States. Roast *cabrito* (tender young kid) is a real favorite wherever it is available, and everyone I know who has ever tasted it agrees with me that it is far more delicious than lamb. The organ meats are used extensively throughout Mexico, where they have concocted some of the best damn sauces you ever tasted for tongue, tripe, and brains.

In the homes of the upper classes, where eating habits are more Continental than native, steaks and roasts are as popular as they are with us. But we are concerned with typical Mexican dishes and I think you'll enjoy the wide variety of them in this chapter.

Señor Pico Beef Brochette Yucatán

> 2 pounds filet mignon, cut into 1¼-inch cubes
> 12 medium-size fresh mushrooms, trimmed of stems
> 2 Bermuda onions, peeled and cut into 1¼-inch cubes
> ½ teaspoon cumin powder
> 1 teaspoon orégano
> ½ teaspoon pepper
> 2 cups salad oil
> Juice of 3 limes
> Salt to taste
> Yucatán Sauce (recipe follows)

Combine all ingredients except sauce and marinate for at least 12 hours. Remove meat, onions, and mushrooms from marinade and alternate the three on skewers. Broil quickly on each side to desired doneness. Serve with heated sauce spooned over each brochette. Makes 4 servings.

YUCATÁN SAUCE

1 Bermuda onion, finely chopped
6 to 8 green onions, finely chopped
1 tomato, finely chopped
2 pimientos, diced
1 tablespoon vinegar
6 ounces beer
½ bunch Chinese parsley, chopped
2 tablespoons oil
1 cup tomato juice

Combine all ingredients in saucepan and heat, but do not let the sauce boil.

Biftec Monterrey
Beefsteak Monterrey Style

During the five years that my friends Kay and Tex Witherspoon lived in Mexico, they had a cook by the name of Inez, who was so good that friends were always asking to borrow her. Biftec Monterrey was one of Inez's specialties. I'm glad Kay contributed the recipe for this book because it's a mighty tasty way to fix round steak.

4 ½-pound round steaks, about ½-inch thick
Juice of 2 lemons
2 teaspoons salt
2 cloves garlic, crushed
1 egg, well beaten
⅔ cup fine cracker crumbs
½ teaspoon orégano
1 teaspoon chili powder
2 tablespoons each butter and oil

Pound the steaks with a wooden mallet until fibers are softened and steaks are very thin. Combine the lemon juice, salt, and garlic and marinate the steaks, turning them over until all pieces are coated with the seasoned juice. Dip the steaks in the beaten egg, then into the cracker crumbs seasoned with the orégano and chili powder. When steaks are well coated with the seasoned crumbs, heat the butter and oil in a skillet and fry the steaks quickly on each side until coating is golden brown. Makes 4 servings.

Matambre
Stuffed and Rolled Flank Steak

Matambre is a familiar dish wherever Spanish is spoken and, loosely translated, means to subdue hunger. You'll need a long roasting pan with a cover for this many-splendored roulade. And plan it ahead, as the flank steaks should be marinated for about 6 hours at room temperature or overnight in order to tenderize them.

2 flank steaks, about 2 pounds each

MARINADE

1 cup red wine
1 teaspoon dried thyme
2 cloves garlic, crushed

STUFFING

½ pound raw spinach
1 package frozen mixed peas and carrots, defrosted
½ cup finely chopped onions
¼ cup each finely chopped green pepper, celery,
    and pimiento

2 tablespoons chopped parsley
1 teaspoon crumbled chili pequín
2 teaspoons salt
4 cups beef broth
Cold water

Have your butcher butterfly each steak and flatten it as thin as possible. Trim off excess fat and cut the edges straight so that each steak is roughly about 12 inches square. Combine the wine with the thyme and crushed garlic and marinate the steaks in this mixture as described above.

To prepare the matambre, lay the steaks side by side, cut side up, so that they overlap about two inches. Pound the joined ends together with a mallet so that they will be sealed as if they were one piece of meat.

Wash the spinach thoroughly, trim away stems, pat leaves dry, and lay them evenly over the meat. Combine the vegetables and salt, mix well, and spread over the entire surface on top of the spinach leaves. Roll up the two steaks, as though they were one, jelly-roll fashion, as lightly as possible. Tie the roll securely with kitchen cord every 2 inches.

Heat the oil in the roaster and lightly brown the whole roulade. Add the beef broth and as much water as needed to reach ⅓ of the height of the roulade. Cover the roaster and place in a preheated 375° F. oven for about 1¼ hours. Remove roulade to carving board. Let rest for about 10 minutes; then cut the cord ties and carve into slices of desired thickness. Moisten each slice with some of the pan liquid (which may be thickened, if desired, with a flour and water *roux*). Makes 8 to 10 servings.

Carnes Asadas Rellenas
Rolled Beefsteaks

2 pounds top round steak
Flour seasoned with salt, pepper, and
    monosodium glutamate

Oil
3 tablespoons butter
⅓ cup chopped onions
6 tablespoons julienned canned poblano chilies,
    rinsed and drained
4 metal skewers

Cut steak into 4 servings and pound with a meat mallet. Dust steak with seasoned flour and fry in hot oil in skillet, turning occasionally, until done. Meanwhile, heat the butter in a separate pan and sauté onions and poblano chilies together, stirring until onions are transparent and limp. When steak is done, place 3 tablespoons of the onion and pepper mixture on each steak and roll up. Secure rolls with skewers and serve with Mexican rice and refried beans (see Index). Makes 4 servings.

Albóndigas
Meatballs

1 pound ground lean beef
½ pound ground lamb
½ pound ground pork
1 slice white bread
Milk
2 eggs, slightly beaten
2 teaspoons salt
½ teaspoon pepper
1 tablespoon chili powder
8 to 10 pimiento-stuffed olives, halved
2 tablespoons butter
1 onion, finely chopped
2 cloves garlic, minced
3 medium tomatoes, peeled and mashed
¼ teaspoon orégano
2 cups beef stock

Mix the meats; soak the bread in milk and squeeze dry; and then blend both with the eggs and seasonings. Form into balls about the size of a large walnut, placing an olive half in the center of each, and set aside. Heat the butter in a skillet and sauté the onion and garlic until limp and golden, taking care not to burn the garlic. Add the tomatoes and orégano, and cook for a minute or two. Stir in the stock. Pour into a large saucepan, bring to a boil, and add the meatballs. Reduce the heat, cover, and simmer gently for 1 hour. Serve in the sauce. Makes about 6 servings (24 to 30 meatballs).

Guisado de Carne de Res
Mexican Beef Stew

4 pounds sirloin tips
1 teaspoon sugar
4 tablespoons flour
2 tablespoons chili powder
2 teaspoons salt
½ teaspoon black pepper
Oil for browning meat
2 large onions, peeled and chopped
4 green bell peppers, chopped
1 bay leaf
¼ teaspoon orégano
4 large tomatoes, peeled and quartered
2 cups canned beef broth or consommé

Cut beef into 1½-inch cubes. Combine sugar, flour, chili powder, salt, and pepper, and dredge beef cubes in the mixture. Brown meat well in hot oil in heavy kettle. Add onions and peppers and sauté until tender, then stir in remaining ingredients until well blended. Cover and simmer for about 2 hours or until meat is tender. Makes 6 to 8 servings.

NOTE: A package of partially thawed frozen corn or mixed

vegetables may be added when meat is done. Cook for another 10 to 15 minutes before serving.

Carne de Puerco Rellena
Stuffed Loin of Pork

A 2-pound boneless pork loin
2 tablespoons butter
2 tablespoons minced onions
1 tomato, peeled and chopped
1 cup cooked spinach
1 cup minced ham
Salt and pepper to taste
1 hard-cooked egg, chopped
2 tablespoons oil
1 cup hot chicken stock

Have your butcher make a pocket in the center of the loin and prepare the stuffing as follows.

Heat the butter in a skillet and sauté the onion until limp and golden. Add the tomato, spinach, and ham and cook for a few minutes over low heat to blend flavors. Season with salt and pepper, remove from heat, and add the chopped hard-cooked egg. Stuff the pork loin with this mixture and skewer to close the pocket. In the same skillet, heat the 2 tablespoons of oil and thoroughly brown the loin on all sides. Transfer the meat to a shallow roasting pan, add the chicken stock, and bake, uncovered, in a preheated 325° F. oven for 1½ to 1¾ hours. If desired, add a can of tomato sauce to pan drippings, stir well, and serve the sauce in a gravy boat. Makes 4 to 6 servings.

Carne de Puerco con Chorizo
Roast Pork with Mexican Sausage

2 tablespoons oil
1 cup chopped onions

4 4-inch links (1 cup, if homemade) of chorizos,
    skinned and chopped
A 6-pound pork loin roast
4 tomatoes, peeled and chopped
6 green peppers, seeded and sliced
2 cups chicken stock
Salt and pepper to taste

Heat the oil in a roasting pan that has a cover, and sauté
the onions until tender; remove from pan. Now add the chorizos
and cook for about 5 minutes, crumbling the sausage with a fork;
remove from pan; drain the sausage and set aside with onions.
Spoon off all but about 2 tablespoons of fat from the roasting pan,
and over moderately high heat brown the roast on all sides. When
browned, return onions and sausage to roaster along with tomatoes, green peppers, and chicken stock. Mix well and add salt
and pepper to taste. Cover the roaster and bake in a preheated
325° F. oven for about 2½ to 3 hours or until meat is tender.
Make gravy with drippings and vegetables. Makes 6 to 8 servings.

Carne de Puerco con Camote
Pork with Sweet Potatoes

2 pounds lean boneless pork, cut into 1-inch cubes
½ cup dry white wine
½ cup white vinegar
2 teaspoons ground cuminseeds
2 cloves garlic, finely chopped
1 teaspoon salt
¼ teaspoon freshly ground black pepper
2 tablespoons olive oil
2 cups water
1½ cups fresh orange juice
4 sweet potatoes, boiled, peeled, and sliced

165

Thoroughly coat the pork cubes in a mixture of the wine, vinegar and seasonings; then cover and let marinate for 6 hours at room temperature or overnight in the refrigerator. Remove the meat and pat dry with paper towels, reserving the marinade. In a heavy skillet, heat the oil over high heat and fry the pork cubes, turning them on all sides until they are golden brown. Pour off the fat in the pan, add the reserved marinade and water, and bring the liquid to a boil, scraping into it any brown bits clinging to the bottom and sides of the pan. Reduce the heat to low, cover the skillet, and simmer the pork for 45 minutes or until fork-tender. Stir in the orange juice and simmer for a minute or two to blend flavors. To serve, arrange the hot sweet potato slices on a heated platter, and pour over them the pork cubes with their sauce. Makes 4 servings.

Guisado de Carne de Puerco
Pork Stew with Green Tomatoes

> 3 tablespoons oil
> 3 pounds lean boneless pork, cut into 2-inch cubes
> 2 cups chicken stock
> ½ cup chopped onions
> 1 clove garlic, minced
> 1 10-ounce can Mexican green tomatoes, drained
> 2 canned chipotle chilies, seeded, rinsed, and
>   julienned
> ½ teaspoon each thyme and marjoram
> 1 teaspoon salt
> ¼ teaspoon black pepper

In a heavy skillet, heat 2 tablespoons of the oil; add the pork cubes, turning them frequently. When evenly browned on all sides, drain the meat cubes and transfer them to a large, heavy flameproof casserole and set the skillet aside. Pour the stock over the meat, bring it to a boil over high heat, then reduce the heat to low. Cover the pan and simmer the meat for about 45 minutes or until the cubes are fork-tender. Pour the juices from the casserole (should be about 1½ cups) into another pan and reserve. Set aside the casserole of meat. Heat the remaining tablespoon of oil in the skillet, add the onions and garlic, and sauté, stirring frequently, until the onions are limp and golden. Pour in the reserved cooking juices and add the tomatoes, chilies, thyme, marjoram, salt, and pepper. Simmer for about 15 minutes, breaking up the tomatoes while the sauce is cooking. Pour the sauce over the meat in the casserole and simmer, uncovered, for about 10 minutes, stirring occasionally. When ready to serve, transfer to a heated platter. Makes 6 servings.

Lomo de Puerco Acaramelado
Glazed Pork Chops

> 1 tablespoon oil
> 1 tablespoon butter
> 4 thick pork loin chops
> Salt and pepper
> ½ teaspoon chili powder
> 1 teaspoon dry mustard
> 3 tablespoons brown sugar
> ½ cup dry sherry
> ½ cup chicken stock
> ¼ cup blanched almonds, finely ground

Heat the oil and butter in a heavy skillet that has a tight cover and brown the chops on each side; then sprinkle with salt and pepper. Thoroughly mix the chili powder, mustard, and brown sugar; blend into the sherry and chicken stock. Cover the browned chops with the sherry mixture; cover the skillet and cook over low heat, or bake in a preheated 350° F. oven for 45 to 60 minutes. Check after 30 minutes and if too dry add another ½ cup of equal parts of sherry and chicken stock. When chops are done, remove to platter. Add the ground almonds to the liquid in the skillet and cook over moderate heat for a few minutes to thicken the sauce. Pour sauce over chops and serve. Makes 4 servings.

Rollo de Ternera
Veal Roll

2 pounds veal leg, cut into 6 or 8 thin slices for
   rolling
½ pound ground beef
¼ pound ground ham
¼ pound pork sausage
½ cup bread crumbs
2 hard-cooked eggs, chopped
Salt and pepper to taste
¼ cup flour
3 tablespoons butter or oil
6 carrots, cut in half lengthwise
1½ cups chicken stock
½ cup sherry

Spread the veal slices with a mixture of the meats, crumbs, hard-cooked eggs, salt, and pepper. Roll and skewer; then coat with flour. Heat the butter or oil in a large skillet that has a tight cover; fry the veal rolls until browned on all sides; remove and keep warm. In the same skillet, sauté the carrots for about 5 minutes. Return the veal rolls to the skillet; add the stock and the sherry. Bring to a boil quickly over high heat; reduce heat to simmer, cover the skillet, and cook for about 50 to 60 minutes or until veal is fork-tender. Transfer veal rolls and carrots to a heated platter and cover with the pan sauce. Makes 6 to 8 servings.

Ternera con Almendras
Veal in Almond Sauce

> 3 pounds veal for stew, cut into 2-inch pieces
> 2 cups chicken stock
> 2 onions, chopped
> 1 clove garlic, chopped
> ½ teaspoon each marjoram and thyme
> 2 tablespoons butter
> ¾ cup blanched almonds
> Salt and pepper to taste
> 1 cup sour cream

Place the veal in a heavy saucepan that has a cover. Add the stock, *half* the onions, the garlic, and the seasonings. Bring to a boil, cover, and simmer gently for about 1½ hours until the veal is fork-tender. Skim the surface of any scum, drain the meat, set it aside and keep it warm. Strain the stock and reserve. Heat the butter in a skillet and sauté the rest of the chopped onion until limp and golden. Add the almonds, and sauté for a minute or two. Place the mixture in an electric blender with about ½ cup of the stock, and blend until smooth. Pour into a large saucepan. Add the rest of the stock, salt, and pepper, and cook for a few minutes over a low heat. With a whisk, beat in the sour cream. When mixture is hot, add the veal, and serve as soon as the meat is heated through. Makes 6 servings.

Cabrito Asado
Roast Kid

You realize, I hope, that the kid I'm talking about is a young goat, and so help me, once you've tasted this delicacy, you'll wonder why you ever thought roast lamb was so great.

From the time the Spaniards introduced the goat to

Mexico, roast kid has been a national favorite. Served with tortillas, beans, and guacamole, it's my idea of a real feast. You won't find kid in many of our butcher shops except along the Tex-Mex border, where roast kid sandwiches are served at every good barbecue stand. However, it is available from some specialty butchers, and I understand it is marketed in some parts of the States under the trade name of "Chevon." Get hold of it if you can. If not, try this recipe with a leg of lamb.

A 4- to 5-pound leg of kid or lamb
2 cloves garlic, peeled and slivered
Chili powder to taste
Salt and pepper to taste
2 tablespoons oil or bacon fat
1 cup fresh orange juice
1 cup dry white wine

Make a number of incisions over the meat and insert the slivers of garlic. Rub the outside well with a mixture of chili powder, salt, and pepper. Heat the oil or fat in a large skillet and quickly brown the meat on all sides. Transfer to a shallow roasting pan and roast, uncovered, in a preheated 325° F. oven for 35 to 40 minutes per pound. Mix the orange juice with the wine, basting the roast occasionally during cooking. Makes 6 servings.

Puchero
Mexican Goulash

Puchero, a Spanish word for cooking pot, is the Mexican answer to a cross between our New England boiled dinner and a Hawaiian luau. It starts out calmly something like a cassoulet and all of a sudden you get the feeling, as you read down the list of ingredients, that the cook had been nipping on the cooking sherry and suddenly decided to clean house.

For example, one puchero recipe calls for beef, lamb, ham, chicken, marrowbone, cabbage, zucchini, sweet and white potatoes, bananas, avocados, chick-peas, pears, turnips, carrots, onions, garlic, tomatoes, peppercorns, lard, coriander, and lemons. If you get the impression that you can put just about anything you want in a puchero, you are right. All you need is a big enough pot.

In all fairness to that particular recipe, the sweet potatoes and fruit are cooked and served separately. The white potatoes are sliced and fried in lard, and so are the bananas. The broth from the puchero is strained and served as a first course with chopped coriander, diced avocado, and wedges of lemon or lime. The main course consists of the meat on a huge platter surrounded by the cooked fruits and vegetables. A big bowl of guacamole accompanies the feast.

The following puchero recipe is fairly basic. You can use any or all of the foregoing ideas. Get cozy with the kitchen sherry and let your fancy take flight.

    1 cup garbanzo beans
    4 quarts water
    2 pounds boiling beef
    1 small ham hock
    1 chicken, disjointed
    1 beef marrowbone
    2 cloves garlic, minced
    2 large onions, sliced
    4 leeks, cleaned and cut up
    2 tablespoons tomato paste
    1 teaspoon crushed peppercorns
    1 tablespoon salt
    8 small or new potatoes
    8 small white onions
    4 stalks celery, cut in ½-inch pieces
    4 turnips, peeled and halved
    4 carrots, scrubbed and halved

8 small zucchini, halved lengthwise
1 can whole kernel corn
1 small head of cabbage, cut in 8 wedges
Garnish of chopped Chinese parsley, diced
    avocado and lime wedges

Soak beans overnight. The next day, put beans to cook in a large kettle with 4 quarts of water. Add beef, ham hock, chicken, marrowbone, garlic, onions, leeks, tomato paste, and crushed peppercorns. Bring to a boil, cover, and simmer for an hour, then add salt and simmer for 2 hours longer. When meat is tender, add all vegetables except the cabbage. When vegetables are almost done, add the cabbage. Cover and cook for 10 to 15 minutes longer or until cabbage is tender but still somewhat crisp. Arrange meat and chicken pieces on a large platter surrounded by the vegetables. Or you can serve the meat and chicken on one platter and the vegetables on another. Strain the broth, correct seasonings, and serve as a first course with chopped Chinese parsley, diced avocado, and wedges of lime, which may be passed separately. If there is not enough liquid, add canned chicken broth. Makes 8 generous servings.

Guisado de Carnero
Lamb Stew

This recipe is a good example of how well the Mexican cook has adapted the culinary influences of other cultures. The Arabs introduced the use of almonds and raisins to Spanish cuisine, and Spain, in turn, introduced these, along with sherry, to Mexican cuisine. Not to be outdone, Mexicans added their ubiquitous tomatoes and chilies. The result is a happy marriage of flavors in this good *estofado*.

3 pounds lamb for stew, cut into 2-inch squares
2 cups (No. 303 can) undrained tomatoes, chopped

2 cloves garlic, minced
¼ cup seedless raisins
⅛ teaspoon each ground cloves and cinnamon
Salt and pepper to taste
1 tablespoon chili powder
1 teaspoon flour
1 tablespoon cold water
1½ cups beef broth
1 cup dry sherry
¼ cup toasted slivered almonds

Combine the lamb, tomatoes, garlic, raisins, cloves, cinnamon, salt, and pepper in a heavy flameproof casserole that has a cover. Mix the chili powder with the flour and water to make a paste; then dilute the paste with the broth and pour over the meat mixture. Cover the casserole, bring to a boil, reduce the heat, and simmer gently for about 2 hours or until the lamb is tender. Thirty minutes before done, add the sherry. When ready to serve, sprinkle with the almonds. Makes 6 servings.

Chorizo
Mexican Sausage

Chorizo is called for in many Mexican recipes but should be used with discretion, for it is very highly seasoned. Our own pork sausage is not a good substitute because it contains sage, which is not a Mexican seasoning. So, if you can't find a Mexican meat market where chorizo is sold in links—or you can't locate canned chorizo in specialty food stores—here's how to make your own. (You can adjust the seasonings to your own taste just like all good Mexican cooks do.) Chorizo is easy to fix, keeps well refrigerated, and it's good to have on hand for some of the recipes in this book.

¼ pound pork fat, finely chopped (optional)
2 pounds coarsely ground lean pork
2 tablespoons ancho chili powder
1 tablespoon pasilla chili powder
2 tablespoons paprika
1 teaspoon coarsely ground black pepper
½ teaspoon each cinnamon and ground cloves
¼ teaspoon each coriander seed and ginger
1 teaspoon each orégano and ground cumin
6 cloves garlic, crushed
½ cup vinegar
½ cup sherry or brandy

If using the fat, mix it into the meat very thoroughly, then add the other ingredients in turn and, using your hands, work them together thoroughly. This is important because the vinegar and the sherry or brandy "cure" the meat and help prevent it from spoiling. When thoroughly blended, store the sausage in an earthenware crock or glass container and let season in a cool place for at least 24 hours but preferably for 2 or 3 days. Freeze what you don't plan to use soon. This recipe makes enough chorizo to fill 2 one-pint containers.

Variation:

For the faint-of-heart, here's a simpler version for a smaller amount of chorizo. While it isn't as authentic a recipe, it isn't as hot or as highly spiced, either. And you can make it in a jiffy.

Just coarsely grind 1 pound of pork and mix it very thoroughly with 1 teaspoon salt, 1 tablespoon chili powder, 1 large garlic clove, mashed, 2 tablespoons sherry or brandy, and 2 tablespoons vinegar. Makes enough to fill a one-pint container.

Señor Pico Presidio Chili

There must be a thousand different recipes for chili beans

or chili con carne, and everyone has a favorite. Here's one that legend says was created somewhere west of the Pecos. We tried it, liked it, dubbed it Jailhouse Chili, and put it on the menu at Señor Pico's in San Francisco. About a year after we opened, I received a letter from a California food manufacturing company stating that they canned a product called Jailhouse Chili and that the name was copyrighted.

Now, I've had enough experience with people trying to horn in on the Trader Vic and Señor Pico names and products, so I appreciate how this company felt about it and we changed the name to Presidio Chili.

1½ cups (1 pound) kidney beans
½ pound ground beef
½ pound diced pork
1 large onion, chopped
1 fat clove garlic, minced
½ cup oil
1 bay leaf
2 tablespoons chili powder
½ teaspoon orégano
1½ cups Las Palmas Red Chili Sauce
1 dried red chili, chopped
2 teaspoons salt
1 cup whole kernel corn

Wash and pick over beans and put to soak in cold water overnight. Next day, in a heavy pot, sauté beef, pork, onion, and garlic in oil. Add all remaining ingredients except salt and corn. Add beans and enough water to cover 3 inches above beans. Cover the pot and let simmer, stirring occasionally, for about 1 to 1½ hours or until beans are tender. Add the salt the last half hour of cooking. Add the corn just before serving. Makes about 8 servings.

Chili con Carne

Here's another good chili recipe. It's quicker to fix because it uses canned kidney beans.

    2 tablespoons oil or bacon fat
    1 cup thinly sliced onions
    2 cloves garlic, minced
    2 tablespoons diced green pepper
    1½ pounds lean ground beef
    ½ cup boiling water
    1 1-pound can tomatoes
    1 6-ounce can tomato paste
    1 8-ounce can tomato sauce
    1½ tablespoons chili powder, mixed to a paste with
        1 teaspoon flour and 2 tablespoons water
    ½ teaspoon each salt and pepper
    1 teaspoon sugar
    1 bay leaf
    ½ teaspoon crushed cuminseed
    2 cans (No. 300) kidney beans, undrained
    2 cups grated Cheddar cheese

Heat the oil in a large heavy kettle and sauté onions, garlic, and green pepper until tender. Add ground beef and cook, breaking up with fork, until meat is browned. Add remaining ingredients except kidney beans and cheese. Cover and simmer for 1 hour. Add beans and simmer, uncovered, for another 30 minutes. If mixture is too thick, add small amount of beef stock or hot water. Just before serving, top with grated cheese. Makes 8 servings.

Texas-Mex Chili

    1 large onion, chopped
    1 clove garlic, minced

3 tablespoons oil
1 pound ground beef
3 tablespoons chili powder
1 teaspoon crushed cuminseed
4 cups beef stock
Salt to taste

Fry onion and garlic in oil until limp and transparent. Remove from fat and reserve. Fry meat in same oil until browned and crumbly. Return onion and garlic to meat pan, add chili powder, cuminseed, and beef stock. Cover and simmer for about an hour, stirring occasionally. When about half cooked, add salt to taste. Makes 4 servings.

Lengua Almendrada
Tongue in Almond Sauce

Tongue is a very popular dish South of the Border, and the Mexicans have concocted enough good sauces for it to fill a cookbook. This recipe and the two that follow are among the best.

1 beef tongue (2 to 2½ pounds)
1 onion, peeled and studded with 2 or 3 cloves
1 stalk celery
1 carrot
Few sprigs parsley
1 bay leaf
1 teaspoon peppercorns
2 teaspoons salt
Almond Sauce (recipe follows)

Place the tongue with all the ingredients except the sauce in a heavy kettle and add cold water to cover. Bring to a boil; reduce heat and simmer for about 3 hours or until tongue is fork-tender. Take kettle off heat, and when tongue is cool enough to handle, remove it from the liquid and drain. Strain the stock and reserve it. Peel the skin from the tongue and trim off the bones and cartilage at the large end. Cut into fairly thick slices and serve with Almond Sauce. Makes 6 servings.

ALMOND SAUCE

½ cup blanched almonds
1 tablespoon sesame seeds
¼ cup seedless raisins
1 large tomato, peeled and chopped
1 slice white bread, torn into chunks
¼ cup dry white wine
2 tablespoons oil
1 tablespoon chili powder
1 teaspoon flour
1 tablespoon water
2 cups tongue stock
Salt and pepper to taste

Combine the first 6 ingredients in an electric blender and blend until smooth. Heat the oil in a large saucepan; add the blended mixture, then the chili paste made by mixing the chili powder with the flour and water. Cook, stirring constantly, for about 5 minutes. Now stir in the stock, bring to a boil, and simmer for another 5 minutes. Season with salt and pepper. Add the tongue slices and let them heat through, but do not allow the sauce to come to a boil.

Lengua a la Vinagreta
Tongue Vinaigrette

1 cooked beef tongue (2 to 2½ pounds)
Vinaigrette Sauce (recipe follows)

Cook the tongue as in the preceding recipe (Tongue in Almond Sauce) and cut in slices. Serve with Vinaigrette Sauce. Makes 6 to 8 servings.

VINAIGRETTE SAUCE

1 cup salad or olive oil
½ cup wine vinegar
1 tablespoon minced parsley
1 teaspoon paprika
1 teaspoon dry mustard
¼ cup finely chopped green bell pepper
½ cup minced chives
3 hard-cooked eggs, finely chopped or riced
Salt and pepper to taste

Combine all ingredients and mix well.

Lengua con Salpicón
Cold Tongue with Marinated Vegetables

This is another favorite recipe of my good friend Kay Witherspoon.

1 beef tongue (2 to 2½ pounds)
½ cup vinegar
2 dried red chilies (either ancho or mulato), or
    2 tablespoons chili powder
½ teaspoon cuminseeds
½ teaspoon orégano
2 bay leaves

Place the tongue with all the ingredients in a heavy kettle and add cold water to cover. Cook, cool, trim, and slice as directed in recipe for Tongue in Almond Sauce. Serve the tongue slices cold with Salpicón (see Index). Makes 6 to 8 servings.

Menudo
Tripe Mexican Style

      3 pounds cleaned tripe
      1 onion, sliced
      1 quart (4 cups) water
      ¼ cup oil
      1 onion, minced
      2 cloves garlic, minced
      3 8-ounce cans tomato sauce
      1 bay leaf
      1 teaspoon thyme
      1 teaspoon marjoram
      2 teaspoons salt
      ½ teaspoon pepper
      4 potatoes, peeled and quartered (optional)
      1 small jar pimiento-stuffed olives, sliced

Wash the tripe and cut into long strips. Simmer, covered, with the sliced onion in 1 quart (or enough to cover) lightly salted water for about 3 hours or until tender. Meanwhile, make the sauce as follows:

In a large skillet or saucepan with a cover, heat the oil and sauté the minced onion and garlic until limp. Add the tomato sauce and seasonings and simmer for about 5 minutes. Drain the tripe, cut it into squares or strips, then add to the sauce. Add potatoes, if desired, and simmer, covered, for 30 minutes or until potatoes are done. Transfer the tripe to a heated serving dish and garnish with the sliced olives. Makes 8 servings.

Sesos con Jitomate y Perejil
Brains with Tomato and Parsley

      2 pairs calves' brains
      Lemon juice or vinegar

½ stick butter
2 onions, finely chopped
1 teaspoon Spanish paprika
2 large tomatoes, peeled and chopped
2 tablespoons chopped parsley
Salt and freshly ground pepper to taste

Soak the brains in salted cold water to cover for 1 hour (1 tablespoon salt to 1 quart water). Remove membranes and veins. Simmer for 20 minutes in water to cover with 1 teaspoon salt and 1 tablespoon lemon juice or vinegar per quart of water. Drain, cool by placing in cold water, and drain again; then slice. Meanwhile, heat the butter in a skillet, and sauté the onions until limp. Add the paprika, tomatoes, parsley, salt, and pepper, and cook over moderate heat, stirring from time to time, until mixture is well blended. Add the sliced brains and bring just to a boil. Serve immediately. Makes 4 servings.

Texas-Mex Meatballs

2 pounds ground beef
2 eggs, beaten
1 cup unsweetened applesauce
1 tablespoon grated onion
1 cup dry bread crumbs
2 teaspoons salt
¼ teaspoon freshly ground pepper
¼ cup oil
Sauce for Texas-Mex Meatballs (recipe follows)

Mix the meat thoroughly with the eggs, applesauce, onion, crumbs, and seasonings. Shape into meatballs. Heat the oil in a large skillet and cook the meatballs, turning, until lightly browned. Transfer meatballs to a large covered casserole and keep warm in oven while making the following sauce in the same skillet.

SAUCE FOR TEXAS-MEX MEATBALLS

¼ cup chopped celery
¼ cup sliced carrots
2 tablespoons chopped green pepper
1 clove garlic, minced
2 tablespoons butter
2 tablespoons flour
2 cups tomato juice
¼ teaspoon salt
2 teaspoons sugar

Sauté vegetables in the butter until tender. Stir in flour; cook for a few minutes, then add tomato juice, stirring until thickened. Add seasonings and pour over meatballs in the casserole. Cover and bake in a preheated 325° F. oven for 50 to 60 minutes. Makes 8 to 10 servings.

Texas-Mex Beefburgers Stroganoff

3 slices bacon, diced
½ cup chopped onions
1½ pounds ground beef
1½ tablespoons flour
¼ teaspoon paprika
1 teaspoon salt
1 cup cream of mushroom soup
1 cup dairy sour cream
1 ounce white wine
8 to 10 hamburger buns
Butter

Gently fry the bacon until most of the fat is rendered; push to one side of the skillet. Add the onions and sauté until almost tender; push aside in skillet. Add the meat and brown it, breaking it up with a fork as it cooks. When browned, blend the skillet mixture thoroughly and drain off excess fat. Blend flour and seasonings into meat mixture; let cook for a few minutes, then stir in soup. Cook slowly, uncovered, for 20 minutes, stirring frequently. Add sour cream and wine and heat through. Meanwhile, split, toast, and butter hamburger buns. Serve meat mixture on open-faced 2 halves of buns. Makes 8 to 10 servings.

Texas-Mex Son-of-a-Bitch Stew

The original Son-of-a-Bitch Stew was a ranch-hand recipe cooked out on the range. This recipe, however, can be prepared at home on the range. You'd be wise to order the beef cheeks from your butcher ahead of time. If unavailable, you can substitute other cuts of beef, but it is the gelatinous quality of the cheeks that makes this dish outstanding. It's great for an outdoor gathering where you can keep it hot in an *olla* (a Mexican clay pot) set in sand and ringed with burning embers.

5 pounds beef cheeks, cut in 1-inch pieces
½ cup oil
3 cups chopped onions
3 cloves of garlic, minced
½ cup flour
1 quart chicken stock
1 cup white wine
1 No. 2 can solid pack tomatoes
1 6-ounce can tomato paste
1 tablespoon crushed cuminseeds
1 tablespoon each salt and monosodium glutamate
1 teaspoon pepper
1 beef tongue, under 3 pounds
1 pound tripe, partially cooked*

Brown beef cheek pieces in oil in a large heavy pot. Add onions and garlic, and sauté until limp and transparent. Stir in the flour thoroughly; then add chicken stock, wine, tomatoes, tomato paste, and seasonings. Mix well; cover and simmer for about 3 hours or until beef cheeks are tender. Add more stock or water if necessary. Meanwhile, scrub the tongue thoroughly. Put in a kettle with the tripe and add:

2 medium-sized onions
1 large carrot
3 outer stalks of celery with leaves
8 crushed peppercorns

Add just enough boiling water to cover and simmer, uncovered, for about 3 hours or until tongue and tripe are tender. When done, drain, skin, and trim the tongue. Dice tongue and tripe and add to beef cheek mixture. Makes 15 to 18 servings.

* It is possible to buy partially cooked tripe from your butcher. If not, it is a 12-hour process and should be cooked ahead of time.

Legumbres
(Vegetables)

Personally, I don't like vegetables. I eat them only because I know they're good for me. But I've got to admit that the Mexicans do some mighty interesting things with their vegetables. Instead of a dab of beans or carrots or what-have-you on the plate, they go for a merry mixup—and the more they mix up, the merrier. So here we go with some real tasty vegetables, Mexican style. Hope you enjoy them.

Jitomate Verde con Queso
Green Tomatoes with Cheese

> 1 medium onion, finely chopped
> ½ cup finely chopped celery

½ teaspoon minced garlic
3 tablespoons butter
1 10-ounce can Mexican green tomatoes, drained
1 4-ounce can green chilies, seeded, rinsed, and
    chopped
10 sprigs Chinese parsley, chopped
Salt and pepper to taste
1 8-ounce package cream cheese, cut into cubes
¾ cup heavy cream

Gently sauté the onion, celery, and garlic in the butter until limp and golden. Add the tomatoes, chilies, parsley, salt, and pepper. Simmer slowly, uncovered, for about 10 minutes. Stir in the cream cheese and, as soon as it melts, stir in the cream. Continue to simmer for a minute or two until flavors are blended and mixture is heated through. Makes 6 servings.

Calabacitas con Crema
Creamed Summer Squash

6 summer squash, sliced very thin
3 green bell peppers, sliced very thin
1 small onion, chopped
2 tablespoons melted butter
Salt and pepper to taste
1½ cups light cream
1 tablespoon grated Parmesan cheese

Add the vegetables to the melted butter, cover the saucepan tightly, and cook, without any water, over very low heat for about 15 minutes or until squash is tender. Stir in the salt and pepper, then the cream. Continue cooking very gently for a few minutes, or until mixture is thoroughly heated through. Sprinkle on the grated cheese. Makes 6 servings.

Calabacitas con Queso al Horno
Yellow Squash and Cheese Casserole

2 pounds yellow (crookneck) squash
1 medium onion, chopped
2 tablespoons butter
1 4-ounce can green chilies, seeded, rinsed, and
 chopped
1 cup grated Cheddar cheese
Salt and pepper to taste

Wash and cut squash into ½-inch slices; parboil in lightly salted water for about 5 minutes; drain. Sauté onion in butter. In a buttered casserole, alternate layers of squash, onion, chilies, and cheese, sprinkling with salt and pepper. Repeat the layers, ending with a topping of cheese. Bake in a preheated 350° F. oven for about 20 to 25 minutes. Makes 4 servings.

Verdolagas con Puerco y Chile
Greens with Pork and Chili

1½ pounds mustard greens, Swiss chard, or any
 greens
1 medium onion, chopped
1 or 2 (as desired) canned chipotle chilies, seeded,
 rinsed, and finely chopped
3 tablespoons butter
½ pound pork meat, stewed and diced
Salt and pepper to taste

Thoroughly wash the greens and cook, covered, for 5 to 10 minutes or until tender, using only the water that clings to the leaves after washing. Drain well and chop. Sauté the onion and chilies in the butter until onion is limp and tender. Add the cooked, diced pork and continue to cook, stirring occasionally, for about 5 minutes. Add the cooked greens, salt and pepper, and stir well to heat through. Makes 6 servings.

Ejotes con Jitomates
Green Beans with Tomatoes

>1 pound green beans
>1 cup diced salt pork
>1 small onion, chopped
>1 clove garlic, chopped
>2 cups (1-pound can) tomatoes, chopped
>Pinch of nutmeg
>2 teaspoons chili powder
>Salt to taste

Wash beans, snip off the ends, and cut into 1½-inch lengths; then parboil in small amount of lightly salted water for about 10 minutes. Meanwhile, gently fry the salt pork but do not let it get crisp; remove all but 2 tablespoons of fat from the pan. Add the onion and garlic to the pan and sauté with the salt pork until onion is tender. Add the drained beans, tomatoes, nutmeg, chili powder, and salt. Cook over medium heat for 10 to 15 minutes or until beans are tender. Makes 4 to 6 servings.

Habas Verdes con Jitomate
Green Lima Beans with Tomato

>1½ pounds fresh green lima beans
>2 tablespoons butter
>1 onion, finely chopped
>2 tomatoes, peeled and chopped
>½ canned jalapeño chili, seeded, rinsed, and chopped
>Salt and pepper to taste

Grated Parmesan cheese
Parsley for garnish

Cook the beans, in a covered pan, in very little lightly salted boiling water for 20 to 30 minutes or until tender. Meanwhile, heat the butter and sauté the onion until golden and limp. Add the tomatoes, chili, salt, and pepper and simmer, stirring occasionally, for about 15 minutes until all the ingredients are well blended. Drain the hot beans, place in a serving dish and pour the tomato sauce over them. Sprinkle on some Parmesan cheese and garnish the dish with parsley. Makes 6 servings.

Chícharos y Zanahorias con Crema
Creamed Green Peas and Carrots

2 pounds fresh peas, shelled
4 tablespoons (½ stick) butter
2 medium carrots, peeled and sliced
2 medium onions, chopped
3 hearts of lettuce
¼ teaspoon dried marjoram
¼ teaspoon dried thyme
Salt and pepper to taste
1 tablespoon flour
1 tablespoon butter
1 cup light cream

Cook the shelled peas, until tender, in just enough lightly salted water to cover. Drain and set aside. Melt the butter in a heavy pan; add carrots, onions, lettuce hearts, and seasonings. Cover and cook without water over very low heat, stirring occasionally, for about 20 minutes or until carrots are tender. In a small saucepan, stir the tablespoon of flour into the melted tablespoon of butter and gently cook the *roux* for a few minutes. Add the cream, and stir constantly until the sauce thickens. Now add the cooked peas to the other vegetables, gently stir in the cream sauce, and cook over very low heat until blended and the mixture is heated through. Makes 6 servings.

Col con Manzana Envinada
Red Cabbage and Apples in Wine

    4 tablespoons (½ stick) butter
    1 head red cabbage, shredded
    1 tart cooking apple, peeled, cored, and cubed
    1 cup dry white wine
    1 teaspoon celery seed
    Salt and pepper to taste

Melt the butter in a large saucepan, add cabbage, and stir until well coated. Cook, tightly covered, over low heat, stirring occasionally, for about 10 minutes. Add the apple, the wine, and the seasonings and continue cooking, covered, for another 10 to 15 minutes, or until cabbage is tender. If more liquid is needed, add a little more wine. Makes 4 servings.

Coliflor con Guacamole
Cauliflower with Guacamole Sauce

    1 large cauliflower
    2 cups Guacamole (see Index)
    Lettuce leaves
    1 cup shredded pickled beets
    ½ cup toasted walnuts, chopped

Wash the cauliflower thoroughly and leave whole (with one inch of stem for easier handling). Cook, covered, in just one inch of lightly salted, boiling water for 20 to 30 minutes or until tender but not mushy. Drain and cool. Place half the Guacamole in a deep bowl and place the cauliflower in it, head down. Chill for at least 4 hours. To serve, cut off the stem and set the cauliflower right side up on a platter of lettuce leaves, spooning on the other cup of Guacamole. Surround the base of the cauliflower with the well-drained pickled beets and sprinkle the top with the toasted nuts. Serve while well chilled. Makes 6 to 8 servings.

Berenjena y Chile Verde
Eggplant and Green Chili

    1 large eggplant, peeled and cut into cubes
    1 small onion, diced
    1 4-ounce can green chilies, seeded, rinsed, and
       chopped
    1 egg, well beaten
    2 cups soft bread crumbs
    Salt and pepper to taste
    6 half strips bacon

Cook the eggplant in lightly salted water for about 10 minutes or until tender. Drain well, and when it has cooled slightly, mash it. Combine the onion, chilies, egg, bread crumbs, salt, and pepper; add to mashed eggplant and mix thoroughly. Place in a well-buttered casserole. Cook the bacon lightly, just long enough to render out some of the fat; then place the strips on top of the eggplant mixture and bake in a preheated 350° F. oven for 45 minutes. Makes 6 servings.

Papas con Jitomate
Potatoes with Tomatoes

    3 cups (No. 2½ can) tomatoes, cut up
    1 green bell pepper, seeded and chopped
    1 bay leaf

191

¼ teaspoon ground cloves
3 peppercorns
1 teaspoon salt
1 medium onion, chopped
1 clove garlic, chopped
2 tablespoons butter
1 pound potatoes, peeled and sliced
Few slices Monterey Jack cheese

Cook the tomatoes and green pepper with the bay leaf, spices, and salt, uncovered, for 30 minutes. Remove bay leaf. Sauté the onion and garlic in the butter, add to the tomato sauce, and simmer for 5 minutes. In a well-buttered casserole, alternate layers of sliced potatoes and tomato sauce. Top with slices of cheese. Cover and bake in a preheated 300° F. oven for 45 minutes or until potatoes are tender. Makes about 6 servings.

Papas con Espinacas y Garbanzos
Potatoes with Spinach and Garbanzos

6 large new potatoes, cooked and peeled
1 cup cooked spinach, drained and chopped
1 small onion, chopped
1 clove garlic, chopped
3 tablespoons butter
1½ cups (No. 300 can) tomatoes
Salt and pepper to taste
½ teaspoon chili powder
1 cup canned, unseasoned garbanzo beans, rinsed
  and drained
Grated Parmesan cheese

Prepare the potatoes and the spinach and set aside. Sauté the onion and garlic in the butter until limp and tender. Add the tomatoes and the seasonings and simmer gently, stirring occasionally, until the sauce is well blended and slightly thickened. Add the potatoes, spinach, and garbanzos, mix well, and continue to cook gently just until the mixture is heated through. Serve with Parmesan cheese. Makes 6 servings.

Camotes con Fruta
Sweet Potatoes with Fruit

The sweet potato is a native of Mexico and is widely used in many dishes of meats and vegetables as well as with fruits.

2 large sweet potatoes, cooked, peeled, and sliced
2 cooking apples, peeled, cored, and sliced
½ cup glacéed fruits (fruitcake mix)
Juice of 3 oranges
Juice of ½ lime
2 tablespoons butter
3 tablespoons brown sugar
½ teaspoon cinnamon

In a shallow baking dish, arrange alternate layers of sweet potatoes, apples, and glacéed fruits. Mix the citrus juices and pour over the top; then dot with butter, spread on the brown sugar, and sprinkle on the cinnamon. Cook, uncovered, in a preheated 350° F. oven for about 30 minutes or until top is browned and apples are tender. Makes 6 servings.

Verduras Mixtas
Mixed Vegetables

1 tablespoon butter
1 large onion, minced
1½ cups (1 12-ounce can) whole kernel corn
1 pound zucchini, sliced

1 canned green chili, seeded, rinsed, and chopped
1½ cups canned tomatoes, cut up
1 cup cut green beans or ½ package frozen green beans
Salt and pepper to taste

Heat the butter in a flameproof casserole, and sauté the onion until tender. Add the vegetables and seasonings and mix thoroughly. Bake, uncovered, in a preheated 350° F. oven for 30 minutes, stirring the mixture several times during the baking period. Makes 6 servings.

Salpicón
Cold Marinated Vegetables

Literally translated, *salpicón* means medley; and this cold, marinated vegetable dish is very popular for festive dinners South of the Border.

Proportions don't have to be exact, so you can adjust quantities to suit your taste. However this recipe will give you a guideline.

1 cup cooked, thinly sliced beets*
1 cup cooked, thinly sliced potatoes
1 cup cooked, thinly sliced green beans
1 cup cooked, thinly sliced carrots
1 cucumber, peeled and thinly sliced
1 Bermuda onion, cut into thin rings
1 green bell pepper, cut into thin rings
1 sweet red pepper, cut into thin rings
Marinade (recipe follows)

Combine the sliced cooked vegetables (except the beets) with the sliced raw vegetables and chill for several hours in the following marinade. Makes about 8 cups.

---

* The beets should be marinated separately, so as not to impart their coloring to the other vegetables. Just before serving, drain the beets and combine them with the rest of the salpicón.

MARINADE

½ cup olive oil
½ cup vegetable oil
½ cup cider vinegar
¼ cup lemon juice
Salt and pepper to taste

Combine and marinate above vegetables.

Zanahorias en Escabeche
Marinated Carrot Condiment

1 pound carrots
½ cup canned jalapeño chilies
Juice from jalapeño chilies
⅓ cup white vinegar
2½ cups water
1 teaspoon whole peppercorns
½ cup sliced onions
Pinch of orégano
1 bay leaf
3 tablespoons salad oil
1 tablespoon salt
¼ teaspoon minced garlic

Peel carrots and cut into ⅛-inch slices. Put carrots in kettle, cover with cold water, and bring to boil. Cook until tender; drain and let cool. Remove seeds from chilies, rinse well, drain, and cut into ⅛-inch slices. Combine remaining ingredients to make a marinade, mixing well. Marinate carrots and chilies for 12 to 24 hours. Makes approximately 3 cups.

Ensaladas
(Salads)

Now about salads. You just don't find our popular tossed green salads served with dinner in the average middle-class Mexican home. First of all, most Mexican dishes are served with sauces made from cooked or fresh vegetables, many of which are basic salad ingredients. Then, these dishes are often garnished with lettuce, radishes, olives, and onions. On top of all this, a salad would be garnishing a garnish.

Now, a hearty salad served as the main course for lunch is something else again, and most of the recipes I've included in this chapter can be used for that purpose. I'm also giving you some favorites from my Señor Pico restaurants, and I hope you'll like them as much as our customers do.

Ensalada Chalupa Compuesta
Tortilla Sandwich Salad

A *chalupa* is Mexico's answer to the open-faced sandwich, built on a crisp fried tortilla. When made on 3-inch tortillas, it is more like a canapé and serves about the same purpose. It can be any size, any shape, and made from Refried Beans, Picadillo, Chorizos and grated cheese, chopped pork, chicken, or a combination of any of these goodies to achieve a sort of Mexican Dagwood.

Here is a luncheon salad built on a fried tortilla. In case you are wondering, *compuesta* means composed. Serve it with cold Mexican beer and a simple dessert like *flan* or coffee ice cream sprinkled with grated bittersweet chocolate.

Lettuce leaves
6 cups shredded lettuce
6 large tortillas, fried crisp
3 cups refried beans
¾ cup grated Cheddar cheese
1½ cups shredded, cooked white chicken meat, or
     1½ cups cooked, peeled, and deveined shrimp
1½ cups Guacamole (see Index)
6 green pepper rings
18 thinly sliced onion rings
6 ripe olives, pitted
6 small ripe tomatoes, quartered

Cover each of 6 dinner-sized plates with lettuce leaves and top each with ½ cup of shredded lettuce. Place fried tortillas on cookie sheet and cover each with ½ cup refried beans. Over the beans sprinkle 2 tablespoons grated Cheddar cheese; slip cookie sheet under broiler until cheese melts; then place the filled tortillas on top of shredded lettuce on each plate. Sprinkle each with another ½ cup of shredded lettuce, then add ¼ cup shredded chicken or shrimp. Top each salad with ¼ cup Guacamole; garnish with green pepper ring and 3 onion rings; top with ripe olive. Arrange 4 tomato quarters around base of each salad. Makes 6 servings.

Ensalada de Frijoles
Mexican Pink Bean Salad

> 2 cups cooked pink beans
> ½ cup diced celery
> 3 canned green chilies, seeded, rinsed, and drained
> 2 medium-sized sweet pickles, chopped
> 1 small onion, chopped
> Salt and pepper to taste
> 2 tablespoons prepared mustard
> ¼ cup light cream or canned evaporated milk
> Lettuce
> Chili powder

If using canned pink beans, rinse and drain well. If cooking the dried pink beans, soak overnight and cook as directed on package; drain and cool. To make the salad, thoroughly mix the first 5 ingredients; add salt and pepper. Beat together the mustard and the cream or milk until well blended and stir into the bean mixture. Chill the mixture and serve on lettuce leaves. Sprinkle top lightly with chili powder.

Ensalada de Nopalitos
Señor Pico Cactus Salad

Nopalitos, the tender young leaves of the cactus plant, are a favorite food in Mexico and are sold fresh in all their markets. Since the spiny parts of the cactus leaves are the very devil to handle, it's just as well that our markets carry prepared nopalitos in sizes from 4-ounce to 10-ounce jars and cans. All you have to do is to rinse them well and drain them well before using.

1½ cups canned chunk tuna
1 10-ounce can nopalitos, rinsed, drained, and chopped
3 tablespoons mayonnaise
Salt and pepper to taste
Whole lettuce leaves
4 cups shredded lettuce
2 tomatoes, peeled
2 hard-cooked eggs
4 tablespoons mayonnaise

Separate tuna chunks and mix lightly with nopalitos, mayonnaise, and seasonings. Place lettuce leaves on each salad plate; cover center of each with 1 cup shredded lettuce. Place ⅔ cup tuna mixture on top of shredded lettuce. Cut tomatoes and eggs into quarters and distribute for garnish on each plate. Top with 1 tablespoon mayonnaise. Makes 4 servings.

Ensalada de Chayote
Chayote Salad

Botanically speaking, this member of the squash family is a fruit, but since it must be peeled and cooked to be edible, it is used as a vegetable. Pale green or almost white in color, the chayote is about the size of a large avocado with a firmer flesh than summer squash or zucchini.

3 medium chayotes
6 green onions, chopped
2 medium tomatoes, peeled and cut into small wedges
1 teaspoon minced parsley
Pitted ripe olives, sliced
½ cup French dressing

Peel the chayotes and cut them in halves. Simmer in boiling salted water for about 20 minutes or until tender. Drain, cool, and cut into small wedges. Combine the chayotes, onions, to-matoes, parsley, and olives in a salad bowl. Add the French dressing and toss lightly. Makes 6 servings.

Ensalada Mexicana
Mexican Salad

3 large green bell peppers
1 medium onion, chopped
4 ripe tomatoes, peeled and chopped
4 slices bacon
¼ cup vinegar
¼ cup water
1 teaspoon sugar
Salt and pepper to taste
½ teaspoon chili powder
Lettuce leaves

Cut the bell peppers in small pieces and mix in a salad bowl with the onion and tomatoes. Cut the bacon in small strips and fry till crisp in hot skillet. Stir into the skillet the vinegar mixed with the water and sugar. Add the salt, pepper, and chili powder. As the mixture boils up, pour it over the vegetables. Serve the salad on lettuce leaves. Makes 6 servings.

Ensalada de Coliflor
Cauliflower Salad

½ cup salad oil
¼ cup vinegar
1 clove garlic, chopped
¼ teaspoon chili powder
1 cooked cauliflower, separated into flowerets and
   chilled
Lettuce leaves

To make the sauce, mix the oil and vinegar with the garlic and chili powder and bring to a boil. Remove from stove and let cool. To serve, arrange the flowerets on lettuce leaves and spoon on the sauce. Makes 4 to 6 servings.

Sauce Variation:

Cook one whole cauliflower, and while still warm marinate it in ½ cup French dressing. Chill in refrigerator. In an electric blender, prepare a sauce made of 2 large avocados, 1 teaspoon lemon juice, ½ cup blanched almonds, a dash of nutmeg, and salt and pepper to taste. Drain the chilled cauliflower and serve on a salad platter of lettuce leaves, covered with the sauce. Makes 4 to 6 servings.

Ensalada de Calabacitas
Squash Salad

6 medium zucchini
1 clove garlic
1 teaspoon lemon juice
1 medium onion, chopped
½ cup chopped celery
⅓ cup French dressing
Salt and freshly ground pepper to taste
Lettuce leaves
Mayonnaise

Cut zucchini into slices about ½-inch thick and cook, covered, in a small amount of boiling, salted water with the garlic and lemon juice for about 10 minutes until tender but still crisp. Drain; remove garlic. Let zucchini cool in a bowl. Add remaining ingredients except lettuce and mayonnaise. Toss. Serve on lettuce leaves and top with a dollop of mayonnaise. Makes 6 to 8 servings.

Ensalada de Verduras Mixtas
Mixed Vegetable Salad

¾ cup cubed boiled potatoes
¾ cup inch-long cooked green beans
¾ cup cooked sliced carrots
¾ cup cooked cauliflower flowerets
¾ cup cooked green peas
Lettuce leaves
2 tomatoes, cut into wedges
1 cucumber, peeled and sliced
Mexican Dressing (recipe follows)

Chill the cooked vegetables and toss lightly with the Mexican Dressing (which may be used either hot from the stove or chilled). Serve salad in a lettuce-lined salad bowl or in lettuce leaves on individual plates, garnished with tomato wedges and sliced cucumber. Makes 6 generous servings.

MEXICAN DRESSING

5 slices bacon
½ teaspoon salt
¼ teaspoon pepper
¼ teaspoon chili powder
3 tablespoons vinegar
⅓ cup water
1 teaspoon sugar

Cut the bacon into small pieces and fry in a skillet over low heat until crisp. Stir in seasonings; then add the vinegar mixed with the water and sugar. Cook over low heat, stirring frequently, for about 5 minutes. Use either hot or chilled. Makes about 1 cup dressing.

Molded Avocado Ring

4 cups mashed avocado
4 tablespoons lemon juice
2 teaspoons salt
⅛ teaspoon cayenne pepper
1 teaspoon sugar
3 tablespoons onion juice
3 tablespoons unflavored gelatin
½ cup cold water
1¼ cups boiling water
Few drops green coloring
1 cup mayonnaise
Sour Cream Shrimp Dressing (recipe follows)

To mash avocado, cut in half, peel, and sprinkle with lemon juice. Press through ricer, then through sieve. Add seasonings and onion juice. Soak gelatin in cold water, add boiling water, and stir until dissolved. Chill until it begins to congeal. Blend avocado mixture with gelatin. Refrigerate until mixture begins to congeal. Add coloring and beat for 3 minutes with rotary beater, then fold in mayonnaise and stir until completely blended. (Add more coloring if it is too light.) Taste and correct seasonings. Pour into large greased ring mold and let set overnight in refrigerator. Serve with the following dressing in center of molded salad. Makes 8 to 10 servings.

SOUR CREAM SHRIMP DRESSING

1 clove garlic
1 pint heavy sour cream
1½ cups catsup
2 tablespoons Worcestershire sauce
1½ tablespoons grated onions
1 teaspoon salt

2 tablespoons horseradish
1 teaspoon paprika
1 tablespoon lemon juice
¼ teaspoon dry mustard
½ pound cooked, shelled, and deveined shrimp, cut
into pieces

Rub mixing bowl with cut garlic and pour in sour cream. Add rest of ingredients except shrimp and stir well (but do not beat) until blended. Fold in cut-up shrimp and refrigerate until ready for use. (May be made the day before serving.)

Molded Guacamole Ring with Shrimp

3 packages unflavored gelatin
2 cups boiling water
2 cups cold water
3 cups Guacamole (see Index)
1 cup finely chopped tomatoes
2 pounds cooked, shelled, deveined shrimp
Francia Sour Cream Dressing (recipe follows)

Dissolve gelatin in boiling water; add cold water and let chill until partially congealed. Add Guacamole and chopped to-matoes, folding in until well mixed. Pour into oiled ring mold and let chill until firm, at least 4 hours. Unmold, just before serving, on round platter. Fill center and garnish sides with chilled shrimp. Serve with Francia Dressing. Makes 8 to 12 servings.

FRANCIA SOUR CREAM DRESSING

1 cup sour cream, whipped
1 cup mayonnaise
1 tablespoon chopped carrots from jalapeño peppers
en escabeche*

1 tablespoon finely chopped serrano chili
Juice of 1 lemon
Salt and pepper to taste

Combine sour cream and mayonnaise and fold in carrots, chili, and lemon juice. Season to taste.

* If the carrots from the jalapeño are not handy, substitute pimiento that has first been soaked in the liquid from the serrano chili and then finely chopped.

Señor Pico Tamuín Salad

4 cups small, cooked, deveined shrimp
½ cup French dressing
4 ripe but firm avocados
8 small ripe tomatoes
8 green pickled jalapeño peppers*
¼ cup finely chopped onions
½ cup finely chopped celery
½ teaspoon freshly ground pepper
1 tablespoon salt
2 tablespoons monosodium glutamate
Juice of 1 lemon
24 lettuce leaves
4 cups shredded lettuce
32 chilled asparagus spears
2 hard-cooked eggs
8 pitted olives, sliced
2 lemons, quartered

Marinate shrimp in French dressing. Peel and dice the avocados, peel and dice the tomatoes, and combine in bowl. Add the jalapeño peppers, which have been seeded, drained, and minced; then add the onions, celery, and seasonings, including lemon juice. Mix thoroughly but lightly. On chilled, large salad plates, arrange three lettuce leaves to form a cup. Place ½ cup shredded lettuce in bottom of each lettuce cup. In the bottom of an 8-ounce soup or cereal bowl, place ½ cup of marinated shrimp and an eighth of the salad mixture. Unmold on shredded lettuce. Do this for the seven other salad plates. Garnish each salad with 4 spears of asparagus. Top with a slice of hard-cooked egg and slices of ripe olives. Serve a wedge of lemon with each salad. Extra French dressing may be passed. Makes 8 servings.

* Jalapeño peppers en escabeche can be secured from Mexican food supply houses or grocers. Ask for green pickled jalapeño peppers (hot) packed with "oil, vinegar, salt, sugar, garlic, onions, carrots, and spices."

Ensalada de Jaiba y Camarón
Crab and Shrimp Salad

½ cup crab meat
½ cup small whole shrimp
2 tablespoons finely chopped onions
½ cup sliced celery
¼ cup sliced water chestnuts
¼ cup pine nuts, toasted
1 tablespoon currants or pomegranate seeds (optional)
Salt to taste
½ cup mayonnaise
Lettuce
1 cup Salad Dressing (recipe follows)
2 tomatoes, peeled and quartered
2 hard-cooked eggs, sliced
Ripe olives

Combine all ingredients except salad dressing and garnishes; toss lightly. Serve over shredded lettuce in crisp lettuce cups. Top each salad with dressing; garnish with tomato wedges, slices of hard-cooked egg and olive. Makes 4 servings.

SALAD DRESSING

2 cups mayonnaise
2 teaspoons chili powder
1 tablespoon chopped onions
1 tablespoon Dijon Poupon mustard
1 teaspoon lemon juice
¼ cup cold chicken broth
Salt and pepper to taste

Combine all ingredients and mix thoroughly. Serve over Ensalada de Jaiba y Camarón. Makes about 2½ cups.

Ensalada de Pollo Mexicana
Mexican Chicken Salad

2 cups cooked, cubed white meat of chicken
1 cup cooked green peas
1 cup cooked rice
¼ cup (2-ounce jar) canned pimiento, chopped
1 tablespoon minced parsley
1 tablespoon prepared mustard
⅓ cup French dressing
Lettuce

Combine the first 5 ingredients. Blend the mustard with the French dressing and gently stir into the salad mixture. Serve well chilled on lettuce leaves. Makes 4 to 6 servings.

Ensalada de Carne de Res
Cold Roast Beef Salad

3 cups narrow strips of cold rare roast beef
2 peeled oranges, sliced thin
1 Bermuda onion, sliced thin
1 sweet red or bell pepper, cut into thin rings

Oil and Vinegar Dressing (recipe follows)
Shredded lettuce
Parsley for garnish
Ripe olives for garnish

Marinate the beef and the slices of oranges, onion, and pepper in part of the dressing for about 2 hours. Drain and arrange ingredients on a bed of shredded lettuce, either on one large salad platter or on individual plates. Spoon on the remaining dressing and garnish with parsley and ripe olives. Narrow strips of chicken or ham may be substituted for the roast beef or you can mix all three and use one cup of each for the salad. Makes 6 servings.

OIL AND VINEGAR DRESSING

Combine 3 parts oil with 1 part vinegar or lemon juice. Add salt and freshly ground pepper to taste.

Ensalada de Jícama
Mexican Jícama Salad

The *jícama* (pronounced hǐ' cama, as in hiccup) is a bulb-shaped Mexican root vegetable, although it is eaten raw as a fruit and usually mixed with fruits and vegetables in salads. Underneath its tough brown skin, the white flesh is firm, crisp, and wonderfully juicy with a delicate flavor somewhat reminiscent of an apple. Jícamas are especially good when kept chilled in the refrigerator and can be peeled, sliced, and eaten out of hand like raw carrots or celery.

3 cups peeled, julienned jícama
½ cup julienned salami
½ cup julienned Swiss cheese
½ cup Oil and Vinegar Dressing (see previous recipe)

1 large bell pepper, cut into 6 rings
Romaine lettuce
Freshly grated Parmesan cheese
Chopped chives or parsley

Combine the strips of jícama, salami, and Swiss cheese and marinate in the dressing until serving time. When ready to serve, place a portion of the salad mixture within a green pepper ring on romaine leaves. Sprinkle with Parmesan cheese and chopped chives or parsley. Makes 6 servings.

Ensalada de Jícama con Fruta
Jícama and Fruit Salad

1 medium-sized jícama, peeled and cubed
3 oranges, peeled and coarsely chopped
3 slices fresh pineapple, cut into small wedges
Lettuce leaves
Salt
Cayenne pepper

Mix together and chill the cut-up jícama and fruits. Pile servings on lettuce leaves, sprinkle with a little of the juices from the fruits, and add a light sprinkling of salt and cayenne pepper. Makes about 6 servings.

Ensalada de Col con Piña
Cabbage and Pineapple Salad

4 cups finely shredded red cabbage
1 cup small cubes of fresh pineapple
2 cups shredded coconut, preferably fresh*
1 cup mayonnaise
2 tablespoons pineapple juice
½ cup heavy cream, whipped stiff

Toss together the first 3 ingredients until evenly distributed, and chill until needed. Just before serving, thin the mayonnaise with the pineapple juice and fold in the whipped cream. Mix the dressing through the salad and serve at once. Makes 6 servings.

* If dried coconut is substituted, soak it in cold water for 15 minutes and drain well before using.

Aguacates Rellenos
Stuffed Avocados

½ cup peeled, diced apples
½ cup finely chopped celery
2 tablespoons seedless raisins
¼ cup blanched almonds, slivered
¼ cup French dressing
3 avocados
Lettuce leaves
Mayonnaise
Paprika

Mix the chopped fruits and nuts and marinate mixture in the French dressing. Peel the avocados, cut them in halves lengthwise, and remove pits. Place each avocado half on a lettuce leaf and stuff with fruit mixture. Top with a dollop of mayonnaise and sprinkle with paprika. Makes 6 servings.

DRESSING VARIATION:

½ teaspoon salt
¼ teaspoon mustard
Dash chili powder
2 teaspoons sugar
3 tablespoons orange juice

2 tablespoons unsweetened pineapple juice
3 tablespoons lemon juice
½ cup salad oil

Combine all ingredients and beat well to blend. Spoon dressing over the stuffed avocados and serve extra on the side. Makes 1 cup of dressing.

Ensalada de Frutas Mixtas
Mixed Fruit Salad

Lettuce leaves
1 large avocado, peeled and sliced
2 grapefruits, peeled and sectioned
1 large banana, cut in 4 chunks
2 tablespoons mayonnaise
3 tablespoons piñons (pine nuts)
Paprika
Limonada Dressing (recipe follows)

Place lettuce leaves on individual plates. Alternate the avocado slices and grapefruit sections in a circle on the lettuce. Roll the banana chunks in mayonnaise, then in the piñons and place one chunk in the center of each salad. Makes 4 salads.

LIMONADA DRESSING

⅓ cup frozen concentrate lemonade, undiluted
⅓ cup salad oil
⅓ cup honey
1 teaspoon celery seed, or more to taste

Combine all ingredients and mix well to blend. Makes 1 cup. (This dressing is excellent for all fruit salads, especially those combining avocado and grapefruit, and can be made in larger quantities, as it keeps well in the refrigerator.)

Ensalada de Noche Buena
Christmas Eve Salad

This traditional Christmas Eve salad varies slightly from one Mexican home to another, but I think this recipe is as good as they come. The Mexicans use peeled, chopped sugar cane or small sugar candies instead of a salad dressing, but plain sugar will do just as well. And there's no law that says you can't use mayonnaise or a sweet French dressing if you like.

6 medium beets, cooked and chopped
4 oranges, peeled and sectioned
4 bananas, peeled and sliced
2 small jícamas or 2 tart apples, peeled and cubed
2 sweet limes, sliced
1 cup peanuts, coarsely chopped
Seeds from 1 pomegranate
½ cup sugar, or to taste
Light sprinkle of salt
Light sprinkle of vinegar
Shredded lettuce

Blend the first 7 ingredients; gently stir in the sugar and let the mixture get well chilled. When ready to serve, sprinkle the mixture lightly with salt and a few drops of vinegar (unless using French dressing), stirring to blend. Serve on shredded lettuce and top, if desired, with mayonnaise thinned with a little light cream. Makes 10 to 12 servings.

Postres
[Desserts]

Mexicans have as much of a sweet tooth as everybody else around the world. Today, they eat cakes, pies, pastry, and ice cream just as we do in the States, though their cakes are usually a traditional type baked for fiestas, holy days, weddings, and other special occasions. Their fruits, which are so plentiful and varied, are often eaten for desserts and are sometimes combined with nuts, tucked into pastry, and deep-fried.

However, their day-in, day-out desserts and, I think, their favorites are the old-fashioned rice and bread puddings and many variations of custards combined with nuts, fruits, spices,

213

and sherry. Sometimes these custard desserts are gussied up by layering them over spongecake or ladyfingers and topping them with whipped cream.

Most of the desserts in this chapter are the old-fashioned favorites and are easy to make. So get set for some good eating.

Flan
Caramel Custard

When the Spanish *flan* was introduced to Mexico, it was love at first taste, and to this day the dessert is a national favorite. The custard can be baked either in one large mold or in individual custard cups that have been coated with caramelized sugar to give the dessert a caramel glaze when unmolded.

One of the best flans I ever tasted was made with ground pecans, which settled to the bottom of the pan and gave the custard a brownish color. It was served plain, but I think that some kind of cream would make it even better. If you poured on some coconut cream, it would be the best damn thing you ever ate. This recipe is basic, but you'll see from the variations that you can add all kinds of goodies.

> 1 cup sugar for caramelizing
> 3 egg whites
> 8 egg yolks
> 4 cups milk
> 1 cup sugar
> ¼ teaspoon salt
> 2 teaspoons vanilla

In a skillet or small saucepan, melt the first cup of sugar over moderate heat, stirring constantly, until the sugar melts and turns into a golden, caramel-like syrup. Pour the syrup into a warmed 8-cup baking mold (or 8 individual custard cups), tipping the mold back and forth and sideways until the inside is entirely coated with the caramel. Let cool.

Beat the egg whites and egg yolks together, then beat in a little of the milk. Gradually beat in the sugar and continue beating until it is dissolved. Add rest of the milk, salt, and vanilla. Pour through a fine strainer into caramel-coated mold. Place in pan with about an inch of hot (not boiling) water. Bake in a preheated 325° F. oven for one hour or until a silver knife inserted in the center comes out clean. While the custard is still hot, invert a round platter on top of the baking dish. Reverse quickly and pudding will slip out. Serve at once, as is, or flamed with brandy. Makes 8 servings.

FLAN VARIATIONS:

Mocha Flan:

Omit the vanilla extract and add 2 tablespoons of rum mixed with 2 tablespoons each of powdered cocoa and powdered instant coffee.

Almond Flan:

Add ½ cup ground blanched almonds.

Coconut Flan:

Add ½ cup grated coconut.

Orange Flan:

Add the grated peel of one orange.

Postre de Almendra
Almond Dessert

3 cups sugar
1 cup water
½ cup blanched almonds, finely ground
¼ teaspoon salt

½ teaspoon vanilla
5 egg yolks, lightly beaten
½ cup sweet dessert wine
A 1-pound spongecake, sliced, or
    equal quantity of ladyfingers

Combine the sugar and water in a saucepan; bring to a quick boil, stirring until sugar is dissolved. Cover pan and boil for 5 minutes without stirring. Meanwhile, mix the ground almonds, salt, and vanilla into the beaten egg yolks and set aside.

When sugar syrup is done, divide it into 2 equal portions. Add the wine to one portion and let stand. To the other half of the syrup, add the egg-almond mixture and cook over low heat, stirring constantly, until mixture thickens to a custard-like consistency; remove from heat.

Dip the cake slices or ladyfingers into the wine-syrup mixture and alternate them in layers with the almond custard in a buttered baking dish. Finish with a top layer of the custard. Bake in a preheated 300° F. oven for about 30 minutes or until the topping is golden brown. Serve hot or, if preferred, let cool to serve without refrigerating. Makes about 8 servings.

Huevos Reales
Royal Eggs

8 egg yolks
1¼ cups sugar
3 cloves
1 piece cinnamon stick
¾ cup water
¼ cup sherry or light rum
¼ cup pine nuts or sliced almonds
¼ cup seedless raisins

Beat egg yolks until very thick and lemon-colored. Pour

into a shallow buttered baking dish; set baking dish in a larger pan of hot water, and bake in a preheated 350° F. oven until eggs are set (about 20 to 25 minutes). Meanwhile, make the syrup by combining the sugar, cloves, and cinnamon stick with the water; boil until sugar is dissolved—about 5 minutes. Remove cinnamon stick and cloves. Add sherry or rum and stir to blend well. When custard is done, remove from oven and let cool. Cut into bite-size squares, and let soak in the hot syrup for an hour or more until cool and well saturated. Pour into a serving dish and sprinkle on the nuts and raisins. Makes 6 servings.

Cocada
Coconut Pudding

> 1 cup sugar
> 1 cup water
> 1 cup fresh or 1 4½-ounce can shredded coconut
> 3½ cups cold milk
> ¼ teaspoon salt
> 2 teaspoons cinnamon
> 4 eggs
> ½ cup sherry
> Whipped cream for garnish
> Chopped nuts for garnish

Combine the sugar and water in a saucepan; bring to a boil and stir constantly until sugar is dissolved. Cover the pan and let boil for 5 minutes without stirring. Add the coconut; reduce heat to low and cook until the coconut has absorbed all the syrup. Add 3 cups of the cold milk, the salt and cinnamon and continue cooking over low heat, stirring constantly, until the mixture thickens and becomes custardy. Beat the eggs with the remaining ½ cup of cold milk. Gradually stir in ¼ cup of the hot mixture to the cold egg and milk mixture; then gradually stir in all the egg and milk mixture to the hot coconut mixture. Add the sherry and simmer over low heat, stirring constantly, until the mixture thickens into a custard. Pour into a buttered serving dish and let cool; then refrigerate until ready to serve. Garnish each portion of dessert, if desired, with a dollop of whipped cream and a sprinkling of chopped nuts. Makes 6 servings.

Capirotada
Mexican Bread Pudding

In Mexico, *capirotada* is a traditional dessert of the Lenten season. Toasted slices of poundcake may be substituted for the plain toast, and ¼ cup of sherry may be added, reducing the milk to 2¾ cups.

    4 slices toasted white bread, cubed
    3 cups milk, scalded
    1 cup brown sugar
    1 teaspoon nutmeg
    1½ teaspoons cinnamon
    ⅛ teaspoon salt
    3 eggs, well beaten
    ¼ cup melted butter
    1 teaspoon vanilla
    ¼ cup chopped pecans
    ¼ cup seedless raisins
    1 3-ounce package cream cheese, cubed

Combine bread cubes and scalded milk in a buttered 2-quart baking dish; let bread soak for about 10 minutes. In a bowl, combine the sugar with the spices and salt; stir in the eggs and melted butter; then mix in the rest of the ingredients. Pour the mixture over the bread cubes and stir lightly until well blended. Bake for 30 minutes in a preheated 350° F. oven. Makes 6 servings.

Arroz con Leche y Pina
Pineapple Rice Pudding

    3 cups water
    1 cup raw white rice
    1 13-ounce can evaporated milk
    1 cup sugar
    1 small can crushed pineapple, drained
    ¼ cup seedless raisins, soaked in juice drained
        from pineapple
    1 teaspoon almond extract
    2 teaspoons cinnamon
    ½ teaspoon nutmeg
    Chopped nuts

In a large saucepan, bring the water to a rolling boil, add the rice, cover the pan, and reduce heat to very low. Let cook for about 30 minutes or until all the water is absorbed and rice is dry and tender. Add the remaining ingredients, except nuts, and mix thoroughly to blend. Turn the mixture into an oiled ring mold or into a serving dish and let cool. Rice pudding may be chilled in refrigerator if desired. Just before serving, garnish with chopped nuts. Makes 8 servings.

Plátanos en Ron
Bananas in Rum

    2 cups water
    ½ cup white sugar
    ½ cup brown sugar
    2 slices lemon with rind, halved
    4 slices orange with rind, halved
    1 teaspoon rum extract
    6 large ripe bananas
    ¼ cup butter
    2 ounces Jamaica rum

Boil water with sugars and fruit until a syrup forms, one that will glaze a spoon. Add rum extract. Split the peeled bananas in half lengthwise and sauté in butter. Transfer banana halves to dessert plates and distribute the sauce over them. Then sprinkle a teaspoon of rum over each half of banana. Makes 6 servings.

Plátanos con Salsa de Ron
Baked Bananas with Rum Sauce

Here is another, more elaborate banana and rum dessert.

8 bananas
2 tablespoons melted butter
½ cup brown sugar
¼ teaspoon ground cloves
2 tablespoons grated orange rind
1 cup orange juice
Rum Sauce (recipe follows)

Peel bananas and place in shallow baking dish. Brush with melted butter and bake in a preheated 350° F. oven for 10 minutes. Meanwhile, mix brown sugar, cloves, grated orange rind, and orange juice. Spoon mixture over bananas and return to oven for 15 minutes. Serve hot with chilled Rum Sauce. Makes 8 servings.

RUM SAUCE

2 eggs, separated
½ cup sifted powdered sugar
¼ cup half-and-half
¼ teaspoon salt
1 ounce Jamaica rum
2 egg whites

Beat egg yolks until thick and lemon-colored; add the sugar, the half-and-half, and the salt, and mix thoroughly. Place in top of double boiler over hot water and beat for about 5 minutes or until mixture thickens. Stir in rum gradually and continue beating until smooth. Chill. Just before serving, beat egg whites until stiff and fold into sauce.

Helado de Plátanos
Banana Ice Cream

½ cup sugar
⅔ cup light corn syrup
⅓ cup orange juice
⅓ cup lemon juice
1½ cups lightly crushed ripe bananas
2 cups (1 large can) evaporated milk

Combine the first 4 ingredients and stir well. Mix in the crushed bananas and let stand until sugar is dissolved. Add milk and blend well. Spoon mixture into freezing containers, cover, and keep frozen until ready to serve. Makes 6 servings.

Naranja Mexicana
Fresh Orange Dessert, Mexican Style

2 tablespoons grated fresh orange rind
4 large sweet oranges
4 teaspoons finely chopped fresh mint
Powdered sugar to taste
¼ cup light rum

Grate the required amount of orange rind, then peel the oranges, removing as much of the white membrane as possible. Cut the peeled fruit into bite-size pieces. In a glass or china container, alternate layers of the fruit, sprinkled with the grated peel, chopped mint, generous amounts of powdered sugar, and rum. Cover and let stand, refrigerated, for flavors to blend. (The mixture will form its own delicious, syrupy juice.) When ready to serve, mix well and lightly pile into dessert glasses, distributing the juice among the portions. Makes 6 servings.

Postre de Mangoes
Mango Dessert

This fabulous-tasting dessert is a cinch to make and you can even whip it up a day ahead and keep it refrigerated.

> 1 1-pound can of sliced mangoes, drained
> 1 15-ounce can of sweetened condensed milk
> Juice of 1 lemon
> Sliced fresh fruit and berries, marinated in a little orange juice
> Pine nuts for garnish

Place the drained mangoes, sweetened condensed milk, and lemon juice in a blender and blend until smooth. Distribute the mixture among 6 small dessert dishes. Chill for at least several hours. Before serving, top each serving with a portion of the fresh fruit and a teaspoon or so of orange juice. (A good mixture will form its own delicious, syrupy juice.) When ready or seedless grapes with fresh orange segments, carefully peeled.) Garnish with a sprinkling of pine nuts.

Buñuelos
Fritters

There must be at least forty varieties of these crisp, thin fritter-like cookies or cookie-like fritters, and all of them practically melt on your tongue. During the holidays, and especially for Christmas, everyone whips up batches of *buñuelos*—even the street vendors. You can eat them out of hand like cookies or top them with a fruit or caramel syrup and serve them for a dessert.

4 cups sifted flour
1 teaspoon baking powder
1 teaspoon salt
3 tablespoons sugar
2 eggs
1 cup milk
½ stick butter, melted
Oil or shortening for frying
Sugar and cinnamon

Sift together the flour, baking powder, salt, and sugar. Beat the eggs thoroughly and add the milk, beating it in. Gradually stir the flour mixture into the beaten eggs and milk; then stir in the melted butter. Turn the dough onto a lightly floured board and gently knead until it is silky smooth and elastic.

Divide the dough into round balls and roll them out as thin as possible into "fingers" 4 to 6 inches long. Deep-fry in hot oil or shortening (370° F.) until delicately browned. Drain on paper towels and shake on a mixture of sugar and cinnamon. Makes 2 to 3 dozen fritters.

Señor Pico Sopaipillas
Puffy Fritters

Here is another Mexican fritter, but unlike the crisp *buñuelos*, these turn out like puffy torpedo-shaped shells. The dough in itself is not really sweet, so without a dessert sauce as in this recipe, *sopaipillas* can be served with soups or with cocktail dips.

½ package dry yeast
1 tablespoon warm water
1½ cups sifted all-purpose flour
¼ teaspoon salt
½ cup buttermilk
1½ teaspoons soft shortening
Honey or Apricot-Pineapple Sauce (recipe follows)

Dissolve yeast in water and set aside. Measure flour into deep bowl; make a depression in the flour and pour yeast mixture into the depression. Add salt to buttermilk and pour into depression; mix only until ingredients are thoroughly combined. Add shortening and mix thoroughly until dough pulls easily away from sides of bowl and from hands. Cover bowl with a towel and place in a warm, draft-free area. Let dough rise for 1 to 1¼ hours; punch down dough and let rise again for half an hour. Remove dough from bowl, place on lightly floured board, punch down, and roll out until ⅛ inch thick. Cut into 3-inch-long ovals. Deep-fat fry at 400° F. until golden brown (turning several times so sopaipillas will brown evenly). Serve warm with honey or Apricot-Pineapple Sauce. Makes about 20 sopaipillas.

APRICOT-PINEAPPLE SAUCE

2 cups (1 pint) Apricot-Pineapple Preserves
1 cup water
¼ teaspoon vanilla

Bring preserves and water to a boil; reduce heat and simmer for 20 minutes. Remove from heat and strain. Then add vanilla. Cool. Serve with sopaipillas.

Empanadas de Fruta
Fruit Turnovers

1½ cups flour
1 teaspoon baking powder

1 teaspoon salt
8 tablespoons shortening
4 to 6 tablespoons ice water
Fruit Filling (recipe follows)

Sift flour with baking powder and salt. Cut in the shortening until the mixture is mealy. Add the water and work into a firm dough. Roll out dough ⅛ inch thick. Cut into rounds about 3½ inches in diameter. Place a mound of Fruit Filling in the middle of each, dampen edges of pastry with water, fold over and pinch edges together. Bake in a preheated 450° F. oven for 15 minutes. Makes about 12 empanadas.

FRUIT FILLING

2 cups fresh or canned fruit, drained
1 cup sugar
1 teaspoon cinnamon
½ teaspoon ground cloves

Finely chop the drained fruit. Add sugar and spices and mix thoroughly.

Nogada
Pecan Cookies

Man, are these little cookies ever good! They're sort of like macaroons—crisp on the outside and chewy on the inside.

1 egg white
Scant ⅔ cup powdered sugar
1 scant teaspoon vanilla
¾ teaspoon salt
1 cup pecans, finely ground*

Beat the egg white until stiff; then gradually beat in the sugar. Blend in the vanilla, salt, and pecans, mixing thoroughly. Form into little balls about the size of a small walnut and bake in a preheated 350° F. oven for 8 to 10 minutes. (Test by lifting a cookie with a spatula; when golden brown on bottom, cookies are done.) Makes about 15 small cookies.

* Blanched almonds may be substituted for the pecans.

Dulce de Panocha
Penuche (Brown Sugar Candy)

This candy is typically Mexican, though it is so widely associated with New Orleans that many people think of it as a Creole confection.

3 cups brown sugar, packed
½ square unsweetened chocolate (optional)
1 cup milk
2 tablespoons light corn syrup
¼ teaspoon salt
2 tablespoons butter
1 teaspoon vanilla
1½ cups coarsely chopped pecans

Combine the first 5 ingredients in a heavy 2-quart saucepan and stir constantly over medium heat until sugar is dissolved and mixture reaches the soft-ball stage (236° F. on candy thermometer). Remove from heat and, without stirring, drop in the butter; set aside until bottom of pan cools to lukewarm (110° F.). Add the vanilla and beat until mixture loses its gloss, becomes creamy, and a small amount dropped from a spoon will hold its shape. Stir in the nuts and pour into a lightly buttered 8- or 9-inch square pan. Makes about 1⅓ pounds candy.

Bebidas
(Drinks—Alcoholic)

While tequila is made in Mexico, it is by no means the only favorite drink of the country. Usually, tequila is taken straight, with a chaser of *sangrita*, lime juice and salt—a procedure you will find in the recipe for Sangrita.

The tall, cool drinks served in hot weather are usually made with gin, vodka, or one of the excellent rums produced in Mexico. And, in the urban areas, a good deal of scotch is consumed despite the high duty.

When we opened our Señor Pico restaurants, we naturally wanted to feature the good tequila made in Mexico. Aside from the Margarita, we had to invent our mixed tequila drinks. They have become very popular and, as I've noticed in my travels, they've also become widely copied. Anyway, we have some dandies at Señor Pico as well as some great rum drinks, and this chapter is full of libations that are easy to make and damn good tasting.

Of course, if you're going to have a Mexican dinner or party, the smart thing to do is to make a *ponche* and save yourself all the work of filling glasses with ice cubes and different kinds of booze. Take a generous guess at how much your guests will drink and make your punch in a big enough container to accommodate all the required servings. You don't have to be flossy and use a silver punch bowl. Get a big enamel can, for instance, then run a rubber band around it and stick some pretty flowers between the can and the band. A little inventiveness lends a lot of charm and a festive air to any party.

The main thing is to buy good booze or good wine for the punch bowl—this is just as important as serving good food. And now—on to some recipes for happy tippling.

Señor Pico Margarita Cocktail

This is a drink served in a champagne glass. The Mexicans call their champagne glasses *champañeros,* and for Señor Pico's we bought some amber-colored ones—Mexican bubble glass—to serve our Margaritas in. It was fun serving cocktails in these funny glasses that came in all sizes and heights and sometimes a little lopsided—no two are ever alike—but it was so much trouble to import them and they broke at such a fantastic rate that we finally had to have them made for us in this country. I still think the Mexican glass has more charm, but they just aren't practical for restaurant use.

In a mixing glass with cracked ice:

Juice of ½ lime
½ ounce Triple Sec
1 ounce tequila

Shake and strain into a chilled champagne glass that has been edged with salt. (To edge rim of glass with salt, rub the rim with a piece of lime; then dip and turn the rim in a saucer of salt.)

Señor Pico Tequila Daiquiri

In a blender with 4 ounces of crushed ice:

Juice of ½ fresh lime
¼ ounce Triple Sec
1 level teaspoon bar sugar (fine)
1 ounce tequila

Blend and strain into chilled cocktail glass with salt-encrusted rim.

Tequila Martini

In a mixing glass with cracked ice:

1½ ounces tequila
½ ounce dry vermouth
Dash of Pernod
1 strip of lemon peel
Green olive

Stir tequila, vermouth, and Pernod; strain into a chilled cocktail glass. Twist lemon peel over drink and drop into glass; add green olive.

Durango

In a shaker with some cracked ice:

1½ ounces frozen concentrate grapefruit juice,
    undiluted
1½ ounces tequila
1 teaspoon orgeat syrup
Calistoga natural alkaline water
Sprig of mint

Shake grapefruit juice, tequila, and orgeat syrup. Pour into a double old-fashioned glass filled with cracked ice; fill glass with Calistoga water. Serve with a sprig of mint and a straw.

El Diablo

In a 10-ounce glass with cracked ice:

Juice of ½ lime
1 ounce tequila
½ ounce crème de cassis
Ginger ale

Squeeze lime and drop shell in glass. Add tequila and crème de cassis. Stir and fill glass with ginger ale. Serve with a straw.

Tequila Gimlet

In an old-fashioned glass with cracked ice:

½ ounce Rose's Lime Juice
1½ ounces tequila

Stir and serve.

Variation:

Add 1 scant bar spoon green crème de menthe.

Señor Pico Potted Parrot

This drink got its name from the bleary-eyed parrot that we perch on the edge of your glass at Señor Pico's and he's yours to take home. We serve the Potted Parrots in what we call a Ten Pin Pilsener, which holds around a pint of liquid. A double old-fashioned glass holds about the same, between 15 to 16 ounces. If you have neither, shake the drink in a cocktail shaker and pour into two regular old-fashioned or any 8-ounce glasses. The drink won't have as much eye appeal, but it will taste just as good.

In a double old-fashioned glass full of shaved ice:

 2 ounces orange juice
 1 ounce lemon juice
 ¼ ounce orgeat syrup
 ¼ ounce Sugar Syrup (recipe follows)
 ½ ounce orange curaçao
 2 ounces light rum
 Fresh mint

Hand-shake liquids and pour into a 16-ounce glass. Decorate with fresh mint and serve with a long straw.

SUGAR SYRUP

Combine equal parts of sugar and water; bring to a boil, stirring until sugar is dissolved. Cover; boil for 5 minutes without stirring. Cool thoroughly; pour into a glass container with an airtight cover and store in refrigerator. For a supply, 3 cups each of sugar and water will yield about 4⅓ cups sugar syrup.

Tequila Sunrise

In a double old-fashioned glass with cracked ice:

Juice of ½ lime
1 teaspoon grenadine
⅓ teaspoon crème de cassis
1½ ounces tequila
Sparkling water

Squeeze lime and drop shell in glass. Add grenadine, crème de cassis, and tequila. Stir and fill glass with sparkling water.

Sinaloa Screwdriver

In a 10-ounce goblet with cracked ice:

3 ounces frozen concentrate tangerine juice, diluted
1 bar spoon Triple Sec
1½ ounces tequila
1 strip lemon peel

Stir tangerine juice with Triple Sec and tequila. Add more ice to fill glass if necessary. Twist lemon peel and drop in glass.

Periquito

In a shaker with cracked ice:

1½ ounces tequila
¾ ounce crème de menthe
Juice of whole lime

Shake ingredients well and strain into 2 chilled cocktail glasses.

Piña Fría

This is a real doozer of a drink because, without the alcohol, it makes a wonderful party drink for kids. If you don't want to go to the trouble or expense of using fresh pineapple, just use the canned. It will still taste great and the kids will love it. And when you make it with rum for the grownups, believe me—it's oh-so-good peachy!

In an electric blender with 1 scoop of shaved ice:

2 ounces unsweetened pineapple juice
2 slices pineapple (preferably fresh), cut up
1 ounce lemon juice
1 ounce light rum

Mexican Presidente

In a cocktail shaker with cracked ice:

Juice of ½ lime
1 dash curaçao
1 dash grenadine
½ ounce French vermouth
1 ounce light rum
1 strip orange peel

Shake liquids and strain into chilled cocktail glass. Add a twist of orange peel.

Copa de Oro

In an electric blender with 1 scoop of shaved ice:

Juice of 1 whole lime

1 teaspoon bar sugar
1 ounce gold rum
1 dash maraschino liqueur
1 dash Pernod or Herbsaint

Blend and strain first 4 ingredients through medium-mesh kitchen strainer into a large glass compote or champagne goblet. Top with a dash of Pernod (imported) or Herbsaint (domestic). Serve with short straws.

Fresa Cocktail

In an electric blender with 1 scoop of shaved ice:

6 large stemmed strawberries, cut up
½ ounce Triple Sec
2 ounces tequila

Blend ingredients thoroughly and pour into large stemmed goblet. Serve with short straws.

Farolito

In a cocktail shaker with shaved ice:

2 ounces tequila
¾ ounce green crème de menthe
¼ ounce Pernod
Dash of grenadine in bottom of cocktail glass

Shake well and pour into cocktail glass carefully so that grenadine remains in the bottom of the glass.

Acapulco Gold

In an electric blender ¾ full of cracked ice:

2 ounces pineapple juice
½ ounce frozen concentrate grapefruit juice, undiluted
1 ounce tequila
1 ounce Jamaican rum
1 ounce Lopez coconut cream

Mix ingredients well in a blender. Strain into a Ten Pin Pilsener (16-ounce) glass. Fill with cracked ice and decorate with a sprig of fresh mint. Serve with long straws.

Bertha

In an old-fashioned glass filled with cracked ice:

Juice of ½ fresh lime
1 ounce tequila
1 dash grenadine
Grapefruit juice

Squeeze lime and drop shell in glass. Add tequila and grenadine. Fill glass with grapefruit juice and stir well.

Changuirongo

In a highball glass filled with cracked ice:

1 ounce tequila
Fresh orange juice

Fill glass with orange juice and stir well. Serve with long straws.

Tequila Collins

In a highball glass filled with cracked ice:

Juice of ½ fresh lime
1 ounce lemon juice
½ ounce Sugar Syrup (see Index)
1 ounce tequila
Sparkling water

Squeeze lime and drop shell in glass. Add lemon juice, sugar syrup, and tequila. Fill glass with sparkling water and stir well. Serve with long straws.

Maria Theresa

In a shaker with cracked ice:

1 ounce tequila
½ ounce cranberry juice
Juice of ½ fresh lime

Blend ingredients well and strain into a chilled champagne glass.

Mexico y España

In a chilled sherry glass:

1 ounce tequila
1 ounce dry sherry

Decorate with an olive and a pickled onion on a cocktail pick.

Passion Fruit Cocktail

In an electric blender with 1 scoop of shaved ice:

1 ounce unsweetened pineapple juice
1 ounce lemon juice
½ ounce passion fruit nectar
½ ounce Sugar Syrup (see Index)
2 dashes vanilla extract
2 ounces tequila

Blend ingredients and pour into a cocktail glass. Decorate with a sprig of mint. Serve with short straws.

Villa Fontana

In a cocktail shaker filled with cracked ice:

1 ounce apricot brandy
¼ teaspoon bar sugar
1½ ounces tequila
1 dash orange juice
1 dash lemon juice

Mix ingredients well and strain into a chilled cocktail glass.

Cuba Libre

In a tall highball glass filled with cracked ice:

Juice of ½ fresh lime
1 ounce light Puerto Rican rum
Coca-Cola

Squeeze lime and drop shell in glass. Add rum and fill glass with cola. Stir lightly.

Daiquiri

In an electric blender or shaker filled with cracked ice:

1 ounce Puerto Rican rum
¼ ounce Sugar Syrup (see Index)
¼ ounce maraschino liqueur
Juice of whole lime
Thin slice of fresh lime

Mix first 4 ingredients well in blender or shaker and strain into a chilled cocktail glass. Decorate with a slice of lime.

Grande

In shaker filled with cracked ice:

Juice of ¾ fresh lime
¾ ounce Triple Sec
1½ ounces tequila

Shake ingredients well and pour into a large salt-rimmed goblet filled with cracked ice.

Jayco

In a large goblet half full of cracked ice:

¼ ounce Amer-Picon
½ ounce grenadine
¾ ounce lemon juice
1½ ounces tequila
2 ounces sparkling water

Lightly stir all ingredients and decorate with a sprig of fresh mint. Serve with straws.

Poncho

In a shaker with cracked ice:

1½ ounces rum
1½ ounces curaçao
½ teaspoon bar sugar
Juice of ½ lemon
½ orange slice

Shake first 4 ingredients well and pour into a champagne saucer filled with shaved ice. Decorate with half an orange slice and serve with short straws.

Rum Frappé

In a champagne glass:

1 scoop orange sherbet
1½ ounces Jamaican rum

Place the scoop of sherbet in the glass. Add the rum and stir slowly until smooth. Serve with short straws.

Acapulco Cooler

In a highball glass with ice cubes:

2 ounces rum
Juice of ½ lime
Pineapple juice

Pour in the rum and lime juice. Fill the glass with pineapple juice. Stir well and serve with long straws.

239

Papaya Cocktail

In a shaker with cracked ice:

1½ ounces light rum
3 ounces papaya juice
½ teaspoon grenadine syrup

Shake ingredients well and strain into a chilled cocktail glass or pour over ice cubes in an old-fashioned glass.

Tequila Sour

In a shaker with cracked ice:

3 ounces tequila
1 teaspoon sugar
Juice of ½ lemon
Dash Angostura bitters
Sparkling water

Shake the tequila, sugar, lemon juice, and bitters with cracked ice, and strain into a sour glass. Add a splash of sparkling water.

El Dorado

In a shaker with cracked ice:

2 ounces tequila
1 tablespoon honey
Juice of ½ lime or lemon

Shake ingredients well and strain into a cocktail glass or into an old-fashioned glass with ice cubes.

Coco Loco

This drink is supposed to have originated in Acapulco and is great fun to serve if you can find green coconuts in your market and if you have a sharp ax or a heavy enough knife to slice off the tops. The coconut supplies both the mix for your drink and the container from which you sip it through a straw.

Here's how. Slice off the top of a green coconut and pour in 1 jigger of white tequila or light rum, stirring it into the coconut milk. If the coconut has enough milk, you can add more of the liquor to taste.

Sangrita

I must have looked pretty glum when I dictated this recipe, because my secretary asked me what was wrong with Sangrita. My answer was, "I don't like it—to hell with it." But maybe you'll like it and, anyway, it's very big in Mexico. So here goes.

You might call this drink the Mexican version of our Bloody Mary, though Sangritas are customarily sipped as a chaser for a separate glass of tequila and served with a slice of fresh lime and some salt on the side. The imbiber takes a sip of the tequila, then a sip of the Sangrita, then a suck of the fresh lime and a lick of salt. Traditionally, a Sangrita is hotter than blazes, but you can modify the flavor of this mix by reducing the quantity of chilies or chili powder.

> 2 pounds (about 6 medium) tomatoes, peeled and seeded
> Juice of 3 oranges
> Juice of 2 limes
> 1 small white onion, chopped
> 1 teaspoon sugar
> Salt to taste
> 4 fresh green serrano chilies or 4 tablespoons chili powder
>   for a fiery flavor
> Tequila

Blend all the ingredients, except the tequila, in an electric blender until smooth, doing a small quantity at a time if necessary. Serve the Sangrita well chilled in small glasses along with shot glasses of tequila and a side dish of quartered fresh limes and salt dishes. Makes about 3½ cups.

Quick Sangrita

Here's a fast, easy way to make the mixture for a Sangrita. Though not authentically Mexican, it's just as tasty a drink.

3 cups fresh orange juice
1½ cups tomato juice
3 ounces fresh lemon juice
3 ounces grenadine
¾ teaspoon Tabasco sauce or to taste
Tequila

Thoroughly blend all the ingredients, except the tequila, and serve in the same manner as the Mexican Sangrita. Makes 5¼ cups.

Tepache

This refreshing drink is famous throughout Mexico. It is a sort of pineapple cider with a good kick to it.

1 large fresh pineapple
3 quarts water
8 cloves
1 2-inch stick cinnamon
3 anise seeds
2 cups barley
4 cups brown sugar, firmly packed
Water

Wash the outside of the pineapple and grind it up, peel and all. Place in a large earthenware crock (do not use a metal container) with 3 quarts water, the cloves, cinnamon, and seeds. Cover with a clean cloth and let stand for 2 days.

In a very large kettle, cook the barley in 1 quart water until the grains burst open. Let cool; add the sugar and then blend well with the pineapple mixture. Cover again and let stand for another 2 days at room temperature until the mixture ferments. In warm weather, this can take from 48 to 72 hours; in cooler weather, a week or more. Strain the fermented mixture carefully through a sieve lined with a double layer of dampened cheesecloth—twice, if necessary. Serve very cold or over crushed ice. Makes about 3 quarts.

AFTER-DINNER DRINKS

Mayana

In an old-fashioned glass with cracked ice:

¾ part white crème de menthe
¼ part Kahlúa

Pour the crème de menthe over the ice and top with the Kahlúa.

Brave Bull

In an old-fashioned glass with cracked ice:

1 ounce tequila
1 ounce Kahlúa

Pour the tequila and Kahlúa over the ice and stir well.

Black Angel

Fill a liqueur glass ¾ full of Kahlúa and carefully float heavy cream to the rim of the glass.

Mexican Grasshopper

In a blender ⅔ full of crushed ice:

1 part Kahlúa
1 part green crème de menthe
1 part heavy cream

Blend ingredients until frothy and serve in a well-chilled cocktail glass.

Drunken Pineapple

2 cups chopped fresh, very ripe pineapple
2 cups tequila

Place the pineapple and tequila in a large glass jar. (Do not use metal.) Cover tightly and refrigerate for at least 24 hours. Strain and serve as a liqueur.

Rompope

This rich and delicious Mexican drink is a cooked eggnog and will keep a long time if refrigerated. It can be made with light rum or brandy, and cinnamon may be used instead of vanilla. Mexicans sometimes add finely ground almonds, about ¼ cup, along with the egg yolks, which help to thicken the Rompope and at the same time add a subtle flavor.

1 quart milk
1 cup sugar
1 vanilla bean or 1 cinnamon stick
12 egg yolks
2 cups light rum or brandy
¼ cup ground blanched almonds (optional)

In a large pan, mix the milk with the sugar; add the vanilla bean or the cinnamon stick and bring to a boil. Reduce heat and simmer gently, stirring constantly, for 15 minutes. Cool to lukewarm, stirring occasionally, to prevent a skim forming on the surface. Remove the vanilla bean or cinnamon stick. Beat the egg yolks until very thick and lemony in color. Then gradually beat them into the milk mixture, adding a little at a time. Return to the stove and cook over low heat until the mixture coats a spoon. Cool thoroughly. Add the rum or brandy and funnel into a bottle or container that can be tightly corked or sealed. Refrigerate for a day or two before serving. Serve in liqueur glasses as an afternoon or after-dinner drink.

PUNCHES

Remember what I said in the beginning of this chapter? If you're having a party, use punches. So here we go with some that are oh-so-good peachy.

Sangría

There must be thousands of different recipes for this chilled wine drink that's so popular in Mexico. Of course, everyone claims to have the original formula or the best—and I've tasted all kinds from good to bad to indifferent. This recipe is our tried and true Señor Pico sangría and if you use a good burgundy wine and fresh fruit juices as we do in our restaurant, you'll taste sangría at its best. Traditionally, sangría is served in a pitcher, but if you're having a big party, there's no reason why you can't buy the wine in bulk and mix up a big batch in a large container.

I've known some people to substitute a good white wine, and this, too, makes a tasty drink, but the proper name for the white wine mixture is *copa de vino*. Whichever wine you use, this drink is just the ticket when you're serving Mexican food or having a Mexican party. It's easy to fix and your guests won't get quite so *borracho* (looped) as they would on hard liquor.

In a 2½- or 3-quart pitcher, mix

⅔ cup fresh lemon juice
½ cup fresh orange juice
5 tablespoons Sugar Syrup (see Index)
1 tablespoon orgeat syrup
A fifth bottle of good Burgundy wine

Stir well.
To this add

1 7-ounce bottle sparkling water
2½ cups cracked ice

Stir lightly and serve in an 8-ounce wine goblet. For decorative purposes, add 3 slices of orange and 3 slices of lemon to the pitcher. Spiral 1 orange peel and suspend from lip of pitcher. Makes 8 servings.

Ponche de Champagne

1 large fresh pineapple
Sugar
¾ cup fresh lemon juice, strained
1½ cups light rum
1 pint brandy

¾ cup orange curaçao
4 quarts dry champagne
1 orange, sliced thin

Peel and thinly slice half of the pineapple, cutting the remainder into chunks. Put the slices into a punch bowl. Sprinkle lightly with granulated sugar. Add the lemon juice, rum, brandy, and curaçao. Mix to blend. Put a large chuck of ice in the bowl and slowly add the champagne. Stir gently. Garnish with orange slices and pineapple chunks. Makes 5¼ quarts.

Ponche Jardín

This light and fruity punch is just the thing to serve for an alfresco gathering on your patio.

4 fifths white dry wine
2 fifths apple champagne or cider with a spike in it
2 wineglasses brandy
1 pint soda water
Sugar to taste
2 apples, chopped fine
½ pound small, fresh strawberries
12 maraschino cherries
3 oranges, peeled and finely chopped
Ice

Carefully mix all the liquid ingredients; stir in sugar to taste; chill. Just before serving, pour over ice in punch bowl. Gently mix in the fruits. Makes about 6½ quarts.

Ponche de Limonada

1 pound bar sugar
1 pint water

2 quarts white wine
1 pint sherry
½ pint brandy
6 lemons or limes, cut in thin slices

In a large pitcher, dissolve the sugar thoroughly in the water, add the wines and brandy, then drop in the fruit slices. Chill until the pitcher is frosted. Makes 3½ quarts.

San Luis Punch

Grated rind of 2 lemons
2½ quarts hot black tea
1 pint Sugar Syrup (see Index)
1 pint applejack
1 pint rum
1 pint port
Thinly sliced lemon

Drop grated lemon in punch bowl and pour on hot tea. Let stand for 15 minutes and add syrup. When it cools, add the rest of the ingredients; chill. Just before serving, add a block of ice and thinly sliced lemon. Makes 4½ quarts.

Bebidas
(Drinks—Nonalcoholic)

Coffee is just as popular in Mexico as it is in the States, and chocolate even more so. The other favorite nonalcoholic beverages are punches made of fresh fruit juices and the *atoles*, which are gruel-like drinks and practically a part of the daily diet for the very young and the very old.

Though Mexicans do drink tea, it is less for pleasure than for medicinal purposes. They have a wide variety of herbal teas, and each one is considered a remedy for a specific ailment, covering every kind of affliction from a sore toe to a stiff neck.

Cold fruit punches are popular in Mexico and are usually

made from the mixed juices of fresh oranges, limes, pineapples, and some of their tropical fruits that are not available in our markets. Many call for the addition of crushed and ground seeds of melons or exotic fruits. Otherwise, they don't differ much from the fruit punches we concoct in the States. So I'm going to skip these fruit drinks and tell you how to make Mexican-style coffee, chocolate, and some of the atoles.

Café con Leche (Coffee with Milk)

In Mexico, the coffee taken at breakfast and with meals is very strong and is served with a pitcher of hot milk for diluting it.

To make a brew strong enough, use a drip pot and measure 4 tablespoons of coffee for each cup of water. Pour the coffee to about one-fourth, or no more than one-third, of the coffee cup, depending on taste, and fill the cup to the brim with hot milk. If desired, sweeten with sugar as the Mexicans usually do.

Café de Olla (After-dinner Pot Coffee)

The Mexicans take their after-dinner coffee spiced and as strong as an espresso, so it is usually served in demitasse cups. The brew is flavored with chocolate, brown sugar, cinnamon, and cloves, making a thick, rich, almost dessert-like drink. Our Señor Pico Kafe-Lá-Té mix (served with or without brandy) is quite similar in flavor, and has proved so popular that it is now sold in jars for our restaurant customers to serve and enjoy at home.

    4 cups water
    4 whole cloves
    1 2-inch stick cinnamon
    ½ cup dark brown sugar
    4 tablespoons regular-grind coffee

In a saucepan, heat the water with the spices and the sugar, stirring until the sugar is thoroughly dissolved. Then add the coffee and bring to a boil. Let simmer for about 2 minutes; stir well, then leave on the warm stove until the grounds have settled. Makes 4 cups.

Chocolate Mexican Style

Chocolate, once reserved for Mexican royalty or those who held high offices in the church, government, or military, is now a household standby, and you will understand why it is so popular once you taste it Mexican style.

In their homes, Mexicans serve chocolate in earthenware jugs to keep it piping hot. Just before serving, they whip it to foaming just as they did in ancient times, with a *molinillo*, a small wooden beater twirled between the palms. Molinillos can be bought in most Mexican food stores, but you can get the same foamy results more easily with a rotary beater or an electric blender. Mexican chocolate can also be bought in Mexican grocery stores and comes already sweetened, flavored with cinnamon and cloves, and mixed with ground almonds, a subtle addition but one that gives the drink more body.

4 1-ounce squares unsweetened chocolate
4 cups milk
1 teaspoon ground cinnamon
½ teaspoon ground cloves
1 teaspoon vanilla extract
Sugar or honey to taste

Combine all ingredients and heat over a low flame, stirring constantly, until chocolate is melted and all flavors are blended. Beat until foamy and serve steaming hot. Makes 4 cups.

Atole de Leche (Basic Milk Atole)

The *atoles* are as popular today as when they originated in ancient times. These nourishing drinks start with a gruel made of masa harina, the same corn meal from which tortillas are made. The basic batter is then sweetened with sugar and usually a favorite flavoring is added, which can be chocolate, cinnamon, almond, coconut, or crushed fruits or berries.

> 2 cups water
> ½ cup masa harina
> 1 teaspoon vanilla extract or 2 teaspoons cinnamon
> 1 cup sugar
> 4 cups milk

In a large pan, stir the water into the masa harina. Add the vanilla or cinnamon and cook over low heat, stirring constantly, until the mixture has thickened. Remove from heat and add the sugar and milk. Then return to heat, bringing mixture just to a simmer (do not allow to boil). Serve piping hot. Makes about 6 cups.

The proportions of water to milk can be varied for a less rich or a richer drink, just as long as the total amount of liquid is used.

FLAVOR VARIATIONS:

Chocolate Atole:

Substitute brown sugar for the white and add 3 grated 1-ounce squares of unsweetened chocolate. Before serving, beat with a wire whisk or rotary beater.

Almond or Coconut Atole:

Along with the sugar, add either ½ cup of blanched ground almonds or the meat of 1 small, fresh coconut ground very fine. (Use the coconut milk as part of the required liquid.) When the mixture has thickened, remove from heat and carefully stir in 3 well-beaten egg yolks. Reheat, stirring constantly, but do not allow to boil.

Fruit Atoles:

Along with the sugar, add 1½ cups of crushed pineapple or strawberries or raspberries or any crushed berries or puréed fruits. Proceed as above.

How To Entertain
Mexican Style

There are two ways to plan a Mexican style party. You can knock yourself out trying to be authentic and cooking everything from scratch, or you can do it the easy way. I'm for the easy way because you'll have less work and more fun. And the more informal your party, the more fun your guests will have.

There are some exceptionally good dishes in this cookbook that are just the ticket for a Mexican buffet dinner or patio party. And the recipes are easy to fix if you take advantage of the canned, frozen, and packaged Mexican foods available in the markets.

Many of the appetizer recipes can be made the day before the party and kept refrigerated until needed. The same is true of the casserole dishes. For a main course, you might serve Green Enchiladas along with Refried Beans and one of the rice dishes. Other good choices would be Presidio Chili, Tamale Pie, or Chili con Carne gussied up with onions, chopped celery, and cheese. A make-ahead salad that would be just right with any of those main dishes is the Molded Guacamole Ring filled with shrimp, topped with its sour cream dressing and surrounded by tacos. Pick one of the simple fruit desserts such as Bananas in Rum.

Indoors or out, the decorations for a Mexican party are easy. Colorful paper flowers and Mexican pottery are not expensive and are available in many gift shops and in all import shops. Another idea is to use your own serving trays and cover them with leaves—ti leaves if you can get them. Baskets of fruits and plants make good decorations as well.

If you want to make more of a production out of your party, get a piñata filled with small party favors, hire a musician or two to play and sing Mexican music, and ask your guests to wear Mexican garb. That should get everyone into a party spirit.

Speaking of party spirits, remember that either Sangría or beer goes just great with Mexican food. If you're having a big crowd, a tub of beer kept on ice or an aluminum keg of draft beer would spare you any bartending problems.

The true Mexican *barbacoa* is a pretty complicated affair for the kind of backyard entertaining we do in the States, where we usually barbecue individual portions of meat, fish, or chicken over a charcoal grill.

Somewhat similar to the Hawaiian *luau*, the Mexican barbacoa is a form of steaming the food and is done in a big, deep pit where usually an entire animal is cooked. It might be a young kid or a lamb wrapped in maguey (agave) leaves, or a suckling pig wrapped in banana leaves, then placed in an earthenware container. A good brisk fire is built in the bottom of the pit over volcanic rocks or porous stones that hold the heat well.

When the fire has burned down to smokeless ashes, a grate is laid over the hot stones, and the container of food is set on the grate. The lid of the container is then covered with a thick pad of maguey leaves, the pit sealed with mud, and a fire, built on the top of the pit, burns for from 4 to 6 hours, depending on what food is being cooked and the age of the animal. As you can see, this is quite a project, and I doubt that many of us gringos are going to dig up our backyards to tackle it.

However, the best tamale I ever ate was cooked by this underground method. Some years ago, after my wife and I had been fishing at La Paz, we flew over to a little town called Tamuin, in the state of Tamaulipas, to meet some friends for a dove shoot. Tamuin was once a magnificent city and the stronghold of the Huaxtecs, an early civilization of the Mayan tribes.

After breakfast at the Tamuin Hotel and before we left for the day's shoot, we asked the dining-room captain, a nice guy named Carlos, if he would prepare a Mexican dinner for us. He offered to cook a Zacahuíl Tamale, which sounded good, so we agreed and off we went on our hunt.

We should have stayed in bed. First of all, we were arrested five times for hunting on private property. Then a typical eight-inch rain blew up and it took us three hours to get home in the downpour. Instead of getting back to the hotel at six o'clock as planned, we didn't arrive until nine, and it was ten o'clock before we had showered, changed, and walked into the dining room. We were sure that our dinner would be ruined, but Carlos shrugged off our concern with a smile and told us that our tamale was a special kind and everything would be all right.

By that time we were the only guests in the dining room, so we ordered drinks, the usual *ceviche* and tidbits, and an interesting soup. The salad was delightful, made of shredded lettuce, tomatoes, avocados, asparagus, and delicious small shrimp, garnished with hard-cooked eggs and ripe olives. The dressing was tangy and not too peppery.

We had just started on a little wine when Carlos brought in the damnedest thing I had ever seen. This, without a doubt, was the mama and papa of all tamales. It was about forty inches long, twenty inches high and two feet thick, wrapped in banana and ti leaves and tied at each end with vines. It was a little brown in spots, so I asked Carlos how it had been cooked and sure enough—it was the Mexican *barbacoa* method—cooked all day underground over hot stones in a mud-packed oven.

This giant tamale was brought to the table in a huge oval bowl, and one of the waiters stabbed it with a knife at one end and ran the blade right across the top. The aroma was heavenly. Then he proceeded to ladle out the most delicious mixture I have ever eaten anywhere. There was the masa, like a conventional tamale, but in addition there were big chunks of pork and turkey, chicken breasts and legs, whole kernel corn, prunes, raisins, and olives with a sauce of chilies, flavored with orégano and cuminseed. It was simply magnificent. Later, I learned that this tamale is a native dish of Panuco, a small village in the state of Tamaulipas.

That giant tamale was still on my mind when we opened our first Señor Pico restaurant, and we finally made it. Underground cooking was not possible, of course, so we rigged up a clay jacket and baked it in the oven. We used a muslin liner and lots of banana and ti leaves to protect the tamale from any flavor of clay. It's almost as impressive as the tamale I had in Tamuin and everyone seems to like it. Ours serves about eight persons, and we have to have two days' notice in advance, but it's a great idea for a special occasion.

Now something you can do Mexican style in your backyard, and real easy at a beach picnic, is cooking in sand. This is a primitive style of cooking that I've seen done throughout Mexico and also at a roundup in Texas.

You get one of those big old Mexican clay pots, called an *olla*, which will break if you look at it, so don't look at it too hard. You fill it with whatever you want to cook, and you put it on a thick bed of sand—not dirt. Then you build a fire of oak, or any other wood except boxwood, and get it going good. Make a circle of burning embers about three inches high and four inches wide around the pot, about an inch or two away from the base. Don't push it against the pot or you'll either break it or burn the food.

You can boil water quickly, keep coffee hot, and really cook this way. But my idea is to precook anything that takes a long time and take it to the barbecue or picnic in the olla and just build the fire around it to keep the food hot.

Let's say you are going to have a party for seventy-five or a hundred people. Make a stand of bricks and put the sand on top. Just keep these little fires going around the required number of ollas and the food will stay piping hot.

Take tamales, for instance. These must be steamed, so put some stones in the bottom of the pot and then enough water so the tamales will be above water but the water will boil and the steam will keep the tamales hot. It makes a nice show. When you lift the lid the steam billows out and it looks like you are actually cooking the food.

Beans can be served this way too, which gives you an idea of what you can do in your own backyard.

Here's another great idea for an outdoor feast. If you happen to have a barbecue pit or a setup, as shown in the drawing at the beginning of this chapter, and if your butcher can get you some *cabritos* (tender young kids), you can cook up the best damn tasting meat you ever ate in your ever-lovin' life.

We were in Monterrey where these cabritos were cooked for us. These were very young, tender, milk-fed kids, and the whole animal was thrust up on metal tongs a good distance from the fire. This allowed the meat to cook very very slowly, as it should to keep it good and juicy. As I recall, the cooking time was about an hour and forty minutes, and when the cabritos were carved, they chopped right through the bones, which were very tender as well. No marinade was used and the meat was not even salted before cooking. You could, if you wanted to give it a nice brown color, swab it before cooking with a little soya sauce and honey mixed with water. Or you could serve it with some kind of a sauce after it was cooked. As for me, I want my cabrito just as is with a little salt and pepper sprinkled on when I eat it. As I said before, it's one of the best damn things you ever tasted.

Whatever you choose from this cookbook to serve at your Mexican party, I hope you and your guests will enjoy it, and—as they say in Mexico—*buen provecho* to you all.

INDEX